FAMILY COURT CORRUPTION

Speaking Truth to Power and
the Consequences Thereof

Jill Jones Soderman

Published by Central Park South Publishing 2023
www.centralparksouthpublishing.com

Copyright © Jill Jones Soderman, 2023

All rights reserved. No part of this publication may be reproduced, stored in a retrieval system, or transmitted in any form or by any means, electronic, mechanical, photocopying, recording or otherwise, without the prior written permission from the publisher.

Library of Congress Control Number: 2023907943

Typesetting and e-book formatting services by Victor Marcos

ISBN:
978-1-956452-46-4 (pbk)
978-1-956452-47-1 (hbk)
978-1-956452-51-8 (ebk)

Dedicated with love and gratitude
To my father, Otto Gitlin, MD
My husband, Kenneth John Soderman, Esq.

Contents

Introduction: *My Life Before the Family Courts*   1

Part One: *How My Eyes Were Opened to the Truth About the Family Courts*   9
    Chapter 1: *A Family in Crisis*   11
    Chapter 2: *The Court of Margaret Mary McVeigh*   17
    Chapter 3: *Opportunities through Loss*   25
    Chapter 4: *Fighting My Licensure Removal*   35
    Chapter 5: *A Yellow Ribbon for H*   51

Part Two: *The First Few Years of the FCVFC*   55
    Chapter 6: *The Early Days of the Foundation*   57
    Chapter 7: *The Fog in Puyallup*   67
    Chapter 8: *Sisters in Crisis*   73

Part Three: *Background of the "Parental Alienation" Accusation in Family Court*   79
    Chapter 9: *Reports of Child Sexual Abuse, with Historical Context*   81
    Chapter 10: *Richard Gardner, the Father of "Parental Alienation Syndrome," in His Own Words*   85
        Promoting child sexual abuse for the survival of the species   86
        On children being sexual creatures   87

On the prevalence and normality of sexual activity
in other parts of the world vs. the Western world   89
PTSD as desensitization   91
Therapy in cases of child sexual abuse   91
More on how the protective parents
should respond   95
Conclusion   96
Chapter 11: *Similarities Between Richard Gardner
and NAMBLA*   99
Chapter 12: *Weaponizing Gardner's "Parental
Alienation Syndrome" Theory in the Courts*   103

Part Four: *Behind the Iron Curtain in the Family Courts* 107

Chapter 13: *High-Conflict Custody Situations in
Family Court*   109
Internal categories of client custody challenges   109
When one spouse is an abuser...   111
If your child reports sexual abuse at the
hands of the other parent   113
Looking for help in family court   118
The problem of "no-fault" divorce   119
The bias of family court judges and their
appointed factotum   120
Chapter 14: *Jaw-Dropping Antics in Family Court*   123
Weaponizing the "parental alienation" theory   123
Which one is the criminal?   124
Equal opportunity enablers   127
Intimidating children with "reunification therapy"   128
Chapter 15: *But What About the Children's Testimony?*   133
Chapter 16: *Who Are Those Abusive Court Actors?*   139
The abuser script   140
The main character: the psychopathic judge   140

    Introducing the sycophants   144
    The "criminal" attorney and the "team"
    you never knew you hired   145
    The lie that shapes the divorce narrative   146
    The protective parent's lawyer   150
    Evaluators and their evaluations   154
    The "therapists" and the documents   156
    The performance drama   157
    Plot synopsis   159

Chapter 17: *What's Going on Behind the Scenes in Family Court*   163
    Follow the money   163
    It is a racketeering process   166
    The stripping of the protective parent   167

Chapter 18: *What We Are Seeing*   171
    Trauma and the effects of trauma—defining torture   171
    From our files   175
    Custody transfer is destroying children   179

Chapter 19: *The Public Health Crisis*   181
    A sinkhole / black hole/ criminal enterprise   181
    The cults and their killing fields   182
    But it's fine   185
    It is a public health crisis   186

Chapter 20: *It's Time to Believe the Children*   189

Part Five: *Onward and Forward*   195
    Chapter 21: *The Story Behind the Defamation Case I Lost*   197
        When the FCVFC got involved   200
        The sisters contacted me for help   202
        The last letter   208

The father's accusation of defamation	211
When speech in the public interest is censored	218
Chapter 22: *Instead of Simply Cursing the Darkness, Our Clients Illuminate the Darkness*	221
What makes our work successful	223
What we do differently	227
Who is our ideal client?	230
A consciousness of the veil of grief, mourning, and profound sadness	236
Those who illuminate the darkness	238
A last word	239
Bibliography	241
Appendix	243

INTRODUCTION

My Life Before the Family Courts

I am Jill Jones Soderman, the Executive Director of the Foundation for Child Victims of the Family Courts, and this book contains horror stories. My clients have experienced confusion and brutal attacks on their character in family court, and these experiences mirror the confusion and attacks I have experienced as well.

*****

I was the youngest of four, born into a family in which my father was an MD, a surgeon, and then a general practitioner who built and owned a hospital in Queens, New York in the early 1900s, along with his four siblings, who were all physicians.

Shortly after I was born, my oldest sister, 18 years my senior, was beset with an illness that was initially incomprehensible and undiagnosable because at that time the medical community didn't have the tools to discover and diagnose this non-malignant tumor. Her symptoms of blinding headaches were initially thought to be "hysterical." For nearly two years, from the time she was

16 to 18, she was treated for a "hysterical" malady and not the consequential medical malady that would eventually take her life. By the time the tumor invading her optic nerve became visible, it was already too embedded in her visual systems to be able to be treated. The non-malignant cranial meningioma finally emerged as the source of what was not hysterical symptoms but the very tangible source of her sudden blindness, first in one eye and then the other. The growing mass inevitably took her life.

Because of the prominence of my father and his family in the medical field, and because of his wealth, the world was his resource in seeking every possible intervention. The world's medical community responded valiantly to the call. Even though there were no tools to diagnose the invasion of illness and excruciating pain, the battle for her life was met with tremendous energy and the search for any and every resource that was available. Illness was the enemy, and the unknown source of pathology was the focus of attention. The focus was also to manage my sister's medical situation and give her a full and fulfilling life. Her blindness was considered a temporary problem that would be solved by the medical field, and surgery after surgery was hoped to provide a cure. It was the age of the introduction of steroids, and steroids did a great deal to manage her pain and allow her to manage her life as a college student until her death at age 21.

My sister's death, while inevitable because of the state of knowledge of medicine at that time, contributed to the body of knowledge about this information. There were never any complaints about a lack of resources, support, or engagement from the medical and personal community.

The focus and work ethic instilled in me was this: if one reached out to the community for intellectual and scientific knowledge and support, help would come. If the tools were available, rescue would be certain.

When I entered the family court system with my clients, I initially employed many of the same optimistic and naïve perspectives. But my ultimate experience was that in this new environment, these perspectives by no means achieved the same results. In fact, to my enormous disappointment, when I sought an understanding of the multiple legal and judicial challenges I faced, I was ultimately brought to an understanding of a counter-process. That is, though the structure and legal basis of resolving a problem do indeed exist, the field has experienced a hostile takeover by a self-serving, avaricious population whose only interest is in self-aggrandizement and financial gain. All of this, of course, is completely contrary to the interests of the greater good that the American jurisprudence structure promises.

* * * * *

My psychoanalytic training began at New York State Psychiatric Institute in 1971 and continued uninterrupted through 1985. As a student, I was assigned to the General Clinical Services unit, the most prestigious unit of the hospital and extremely well-funded. It attracted the most famous and skilled psychiatrists and psychoanalysts in the world: Dr. Otto Kernberg, for example, was renowned for his work in the area of borderline personality disorder; Dr. Harold Searles was renowned for his unique skills in treating borderline and schizophrenic patients; and Dr. Hugh Buttry was a pioneer in the field of addressing racial discrimination in the psychiatric community. My supervisors came from among these outstanding men.

When I worked in the hospital, these doctors referred patients to me.

Shortly after my student training period, I was employed at NYSPI full-time as a clinical supervisor for the residents and interns for the General Clinical Services. After becoming licensed in clinical social work in New York and New Jersey, I engaged in analytic institute training programs in both states, lectured in social work, and was appointed as a Psychiatric Institutional Review Board member.

My ongoing training included classwork supervision and clinical treatment of patients in two institutes in New York and New Jersey, as well as attending relevant coursework at Lennox Hill Hospital and Fifth Avenue Hospital. This included a two-year program in human sexuality, normal and abnormal, which included child sexual abuse.

In 1980 I enrolled in an independent study program recommended to me by others at the New York State Psychiatric Institute. My understanding was that the compendium of my disparate academic work would be coordinated and accredited for the program to award me a doctorate in psychoanalysis. I completed the program and graduated in 1985.

After marrying in 1985, I moved into private practice, continuing to work as a psychotherapist and psychoanalyst. Though my workload was reduced, I still engaged professionally with the New York State Psychiatric Institute.

My entrance into the family court system was as a therapeutic professional rather than as a litigant, but like many of my clients, I came into it naïve. Though I had never had personal experience with the courts on any level, I had been educated in civics and social processes. I was a citizen of the United States. Surely, I knew what to expect.

My life was entirely normal and well-organized. By 1994 I was a widowed mother and a provider of psychotherapeutic services, with 23 years of unimpeachable work and never a complaint of any kind from anyone. I was an adjunct at the New York State Psychiatric Institute, a supervisor, a clinician, and a source of referrals for the most challenging of cases. My life made sense, with no disputes or controversy in my field of study and practice. And this took place when I was working in the most difficult areas, the biologically depressed population, with their high suicide rates. My clients were the ones whose treatment had failed out of psychotherapy, ECT, implants, psychopharmacology, and other treatments. Others who worked with this population inevitably had clients who killed themselves, but none of my clients committed suicide or harmed themselves. This unusual level of success with my long-term clients was directly related to the level of care these clients received.

When I walked into family court, I entered a world that I thought was simply a dimension of my professional life. I was a professional practitioner attempting to resolve a problem that I was professionally, educationally, and by licensure well equipped to do. I thought I would be working in synchrony with, and in support of, the court as an advisor to help them better understand the children's circumstances. Because these children were my clients, I understood them well, after having scores of hours of interacting with them.

However, I found myself in a world that I never could have expected or anticipated. I was completely unprepared for it. This world of the family court made no sense, nothing about it made sense; I didn't know what it meant. At first, I reasoned it must be because of my lack of familiarity with it. It was my lack of experience, it was because of me, not because of them.

I didn't know then that behind the scenes there was an entire fabric from top to bottom of financial exploitation, complete power over people's lives, and no redress to that authority.

I became one of their targets. I was to find myself stripped of my credentials based on multiple false allegations with no means of redress.

This is the experience of most protective parents. You come into the court system naïve, innocent, and simply in need of the services of a court that you expect to work toward justice and truth. It is a public entity, a government authority, and it seems normal. Then you find out you're in a world that seems irrational beyond your comprehension. Like me, you feel like you must not be understanding something. It must be your fault for misperceiving what's going on. Eventually, you find that you are a victim of a system that you never even knew existed. You find a deep, dark, malevolent corruption on every level of authority that is counter to all constitutional guarantees of life, liberty, and the pursuit of happiness.

Walking into the family court is like walking into the twilight zone, like walking from day into night. It took an awakening for me to understand that dealing with family court authorities is like dealing with the grip of a boa constrictor.

* * * * *

In the medical world, the disease was the enemy, and people came together. In the family court system, the enemies are the people themselves. They have perverted the system to their own avaricious desires.

In the family court system, I experienced a dawning understanding, a coming to consciousness of this sickness within our society, and then a determination to combat it. This I am accomplishing through the Foundation for Child Victims of the Family Courts, which is based on a psychoanalytic understanding of human dynamics and social processes.

Each case that the FCVFC takes on is one that we purpose to speak to the bigger picture. Each case is designed to address global concerns. With each case, we seek to create an awareness of the tragedies and challenges created by the corruption we face.

PART ONE

How My Eyes Were Opened to the Truth About the Family Courts

Chapter 1

A Family in Crisis

In 1999 I volunteered as a social worker at Strengthen our Sisters, a domestic violence shelter in West Milford, New Jersey. On my first day there, I talked a teenager back from the window where she was going to jump.

Afterward, I talked with a volunteer in a burka. Though I couldn't see her face, I could read at least some of her body language—the movement of her arms and head—and could hear the tone of her voice. Her accent was American, and she had a lilting voice, a lovely soft voice, punctuated with humor and sarcasm. I learned that she was from the Midwest rather than the Middle East. Her name was Shannon.[1]

Shannon told me her boys needed help and asked me to come to visit while their father was away on business in Egypt. Then she slipped off her burka to show me her black eye, and I knew she needed help too.

She didn't have any money, but that didn't matter. The next day I parked my Mercedes and walked up to her apartment in the inner-city area of Patterson, New Jersey.

---

[1] Throughout this book, pseudonyms are used to protect confidentiality.

I saw a little boy, about 7, peeking out the door. Shannon also peeked out the door and then opened it just wide enough to let me in. No burka today, she was rather in jeans and a t-shirt. The black eye still made me wince. She introduced her three boys by their Middle Eastern names. The younger ones must have been about 5 and 3. They enjoyed showing me their cars, and when it was time for me to go, the oldest, Rashad, ran out to the vacant lot next door, where I saw a lone tulip growing. He picked it and ran back to hand it to me. I still have that tulip.

Shannon stood with me a few moments longer telling me just a little about how her husband had beaten her with a 2x4 and put her in the hospital. Subsequently, I reviewed medical records, police reports, and photographs that revealed beatings that were so brutal that the woman before me was unidentifiable. Her eyes were swollen shut and her face so black and blue that if it weren't for pieces of her blonde hair and the medical record identification, I would not have known who she was. Her entire body was hematoma-colored: black and purple, and it was photographed for a police report as part of a forensic evaluation.

The next week when I saw Shannon at the women's shelter, she let me know it was safe to visit again—her husband was still on a business trip in Egypt. She didn't even know what he did there. When she asked about it, he yelled at her.

This time when I came to visit, the little boys were ready to show me more than cars. They ran to the bedroom, yelling, as I followed. By the time I reached it, Rashad was already in the closet pulling out a big suitcase. It was the one their father zipped them up in and left them in, one of them said, jumping up and down. They showed me the hooks he hung them on, upside down. They showed me the window he climbed in to enter their bedrooms and frighten them. Rashad said something about burning down a building.

Shannon explained that the first time she had tried to leave her husband, he had set their apartment on fire. It was never proven that he did it, but he had threatened her with his skill as an arsonist. They had all gotten out, but at five years old, Rashad had been blamed for the fire.

I steeled myself with determination and invited everyone over to my very child-friendly home office, telling them about my trampoline, swimming pool, woods, and stream. Shannon decided it would be worth the risk, even though she didn't know when he would return. That was the beginning of therapy at my house for a year for all three boys and their mother. They would play on the trampoline until they were exhausted, and then they'd come in and I'd feed them all. Then they played indoors and did therapy by turns. Every time Shannon came and removed her burka, she was purposefully transformed from the Middle East to Middle America, in jeans, a t-shirt, and sneakers.

This blonde, blue-eyed mother from Nebraska had a father who would also beat her mother and throw her out of the house after stripping her naked. In childhood, Shannon had become the replacement for her mother, massaging her father's feet and shining his shoes. She had stood in awe of him, the brilliant, powerful, wealthy businessman. Then she finally escaped and married someone who seemed very different from her Midwestern father: a Middle Easterner who had been a respected pediatrician back in Egypt but in America claimed to be just a taxicab driver. It didn't take long for her to find that she had run from a brutally abusive father into the arms of another brutal abuser. Here was a twentieth-century American woman, marrying a man whose culture and personal ethics were completely antithetical to female autonomy in the twentieth-century United States.

I got the photos from the hospital that showed Shannon's beaten body. They would be one more piece in the ironclad case I was making to show the family courts that her husband was a terrorist abuser.[2] I already had photos of the hooks in the apartment where he hung his sons and of the outside wall of the apartment building where he climbed up to the window next to the vacant lot without any street lights exposing him.

Taking on the role of volunteer forensic advocate with a vengeance, I interviewed neighbors, teachers, friends, medical professionals, and others. I found 37 who were willing to testify in court if they needed to, and I got each of them to write sworn affidavits. Yes, it was an open-and-shut case.

Eventually, with a mountain of evidence, I was able to help Shannon get a protective order and get to a safe house. I arranged for psychopharmacological intervention and continued to engage them in intensive therapy sessions.

Finally, her divorce was finalized. There was no doubt in my mind at all that she would get full custody of these children and the abuser would be out of their lives forever. I interacted with her sister and other members of her family, and they agreed to welcome her back. They even

---

2   See Appendix Document 1

CHAPTER 1

offered to help buy her plane tickets to get her back to Nebraska.

Off to family court we went—armed with my mountains of utterly compelling evidence. I had no official position, but I was a fierce and determined advocate for this little family.

And I was right again. The judge's gavel banged down, ordering full custody of all three children to go to Shannon and giving her permission to leave the area. She threw her arms around me and thanked me, promising to buy her plane tickets immediately.

But the victory was short-lived. I had no idea how the family court system really worked. Or that a protective parent can never be sure of her children's safety until they're not children anymore—or their abuser is dead.

Chapter 2

The Court of Margaret Mary McVeigh

In the spring of 2000, a year after I had met them, Shannon and her boys were ready to fly to Nebraska. They were happy and excited. But we weren't able to move fast enough, and their world came crashing down.

Two days before their early morning flight, Shannon was notified that the abuser had gotten his own protective order—against her. He had "applied for reconsideration," charging Shannon with the fraudulent term "parental alienation," saying that everything she had claimed about him was untrue and she had planted lies in her sons' heads. He wanted full custody transferred to him and asked for a different judge.

He got it. Judge Margaret Mary McVeigh was assigned to the case, which was scheduled for the following Monday. The court papers said that one Paul Dasher was being appointed to evaluate the case for parental alienation.

I saw this hearing as only an interruption to the way forward. I assumed that Paul Dasher was a colleague who would be responsive to the evidence I was ready to provide and the many witnesses, including myself, who were ready to speak.

But as experience would inform us, this was the beginning of the end of any hope for the rescue of the children, the undermining of all of my efforts on this family's behalf, and the demise of my career. The gates of hell were opening, and I walked through them completely oblivious to the devastation of all of our lives that was to follow.

Monday came. I went to court and met Shannon, who was there with her three little boys. The waiting room was crowded with people in suits milling around, murmuring to each other, and sitting pensively. Across the room, there was the children's father, tall and thin, dressed in dark suit pants, a white shirt with rolled-up sleeves, and a tie. His long, thick, heavy beard was the only indication of his foreignness. He stood with three attorneys and three Middle-Eastern-looking men, one with a briefcase. Shannon had told me he was always driving around with two or three other Middle Easterners.

I sat with the children, their mother, and the witnesses who joined us in the court waiting room. Any minute we expected to be called into the hearing with the family, where I would be present as a spectator.

While we were waiting, one of the attorneys who had been standing with the children's father motioned to me to join him with two other attorneys in the hallway outside the doors leading to the courtroom of Judge Margaret Mary McVeigh. The three attorneys surrounded me, introduced themselves, and stated without hesitation, without pause, that if I testified in this case, I would never work in my profession again. Each of them in turn briefly stated that my presence was not welcome and that they wanted me gone immediately, if not sooner. They wanted me to just walk out the door and never be seen or heard from again.

CHAPTER 2

Surrounded by them and sequestered in the hallway outside of the courtroom of Judge Margaret Mary McVeigh, I reached for my cell phone in my pocket, flipped it open, and dialed my secretary. As I did so, I said to them, "I am calling the state attorney general's office, and I am reporting you for threats and attempts of intimidation against a witness. Right now, I am going to dictate a letter to my secretary who will be sending this to the proper authorities, to report you for attempting to threaten me, and interfering with my whistleblower status as a mandated reporter. When I'm finished with sending this letter to the state's attorney general, I will be contacting the administration of the court to report to Judge Margaret Mary McVeigh for witness threats and intimidation."

At that moment, in that setting, I dictated a letter to my secretary who then faxed and mailed it to Inspector Cresenz.[3] I also filed a verbal complaint with the office of the court administration, and later I had my secretary fax my complaint to the administration of the courts in Patterson, New Jersey. The person I spoke with at the administration of the courts told me to contact the secretary of Judge Margaret Mary McVeigh and inform her of the experience of threats and intimidation. All this, I did within a short time of this interaction with these threatening attorneys.

As I was beginning to dictate these letters, their parting words to me were, "You will never work in your profession again." I said, "We will see who has the last word in this matter." The three lawyers walked away, and

---

3   See Appendix, Document 2

not long after I saw them meeting with Paul Dasher, the case evaluator. As soon as the attorneys were finished meeting with him, I introduced myself to Paul Dasher and told him I had information that I believed was important for him to be aware of. He said, "Send me what you want me to see." A brief handwritten note introduced myself and offered a few words of defense for this family.[4] I also included some text that I had sent to Saint Clare's hospital when the oldest son had been admitted there for acute suicidality.

As we sat and waited, the little boys became increasingly restless. One of them crawled under a table where the Middle Easterner's briefcase lay, flipped it open a tiny bit, and closed it again. I saw batches of bills inside. It appeared to be filled with money.

There was no court hearing that day. That was Monday. For the rest of the week, we came to the courthouse at 9 in the morning, expecting to appear at a court hearing to present our witnesses. Each day there was no hearing. Each day one or two of the witnesses dropped out. By Friday no witnesses appeared, though I had their sworn affidavits in my possession.[5] As of Friday, it was clear that no court hearing would be entertained.

Soon after that week of no hearings, I negotiated to meet with Shannon and her husband together, confidentially, without consequences to him, to see if terms

---

[4] See Appendix, Document 3

[5] It was only years later in discovery, when I brought a lawsuit against those who sought my license removal, that I found that this informal handwritten note was made out to be something it was not, and was used against me. Appendix Document 4 shows how Judge Margaret Mary McVeigh represented this handwritten note as being something far different from what it actually was.

CHAPTER 2

could be mediated and if something could be done. They came to my home one evening, from 8 in the evening to 1 in the morning. As the hours wore on, pizza and sodas being consumed, Shannon began to remove pieces of her burka, until she finally sat before me, transformed once again, in a cotton t-shirt, bright blue slacks, and sneakers.

I thought the husband looked very much like Ayatollah Khomeini, with his heavy beard, heavy eyebrows, and fierce eyes. Mostly, he spoke in Arabic to Shannon, who answered him in Arabic. He sat glaring at me with the Koran in his lap speaking at me in Arabic, perhaps cursing me. I had wanted to make progress with him, but except for this, he barely spoke to me.

I learned that the three boys were to be seen in interviews and evaluated by Paul Dasher. However, I later learned that this court-appointed so-called evaluator never met with the children. They described being present at Paul Dasher's home when he met with their father. These two men would speak for an extended period while the children were ignored, never being seen or questioned by him at all. The children were extremely hyperactive, hypersensitive, hypervigilant, uninhibited in their communications, and with a great deal to say. They were eager to speak to Paul Dasher, but each of them told me that he seemed to have no interest whatsoever in speaking to them. As far as I was ever able to discern, Paul Dasher did not ever speak with them.

Shannon decided to move forward with a court-appointed attorney instead of working pro se, and the attorney didn't contact me, so I stepped back from the case. Eventually, a hearing took place, but I was not present for it.

Based on Paul Dasher's report that the mother was culpable of "parental alienation," Judge Margaret Mary McVeigh ordered that the custody of the children be transferred away from their mother to Child Protective Services. CPS then decided that the children would be placed in the residence of the father and then assigned various services to the family, thus being able to bill the government for services to special needs children.

This order caused absolute hysterics and revolt from the children.

The pickup order written by the father's attorney included the directive that the police were to use "all necessary force"[6] in removing the children from the custody of their mother into the custody of the father. At the front door of the children's apartment in Patterson, with a bag packed by their mother who was forced into compliance, the three little boys took off running down the street to evade capture. I was present for this scene, as three policemen built like sumo wrestlers chased three little boys down the side streets in various directions. As they were running frantically the police yelled to me, "Why aren't you taping this scene?" They couldn't believe they were being forced to chase and capture little children. However, they did indeed round them up and then hustle them into a car with the father and his minions. The children appeared completely broken.

The oldest child, the child most articulate and vociferous in his complaints against the court, became acutely suicidal. He was hospitalized, beginning a long series of hospitalizations at Saint Clare's Hospital. As

---

6 See Appendix, Document 5

Rashad's time passed in the "quiet room," his screams and laments could be heard through the halls and even through phone lines as staff were on calls.

I later did some research on Richard Gruber, the attorney who led in executing the father's demand that the children be placed in "treatment," clearing orders for the use of psychotropic, black-box-warning medications. This same Richard Gruber, who seemed to enjoy showing off his ice-cubed-size diamond cufflinks and talking rudely to the elderly black secretary, was one of the three attorneys who had accosted me in the hallway. A few years later I would learn that he was disbarred for malpractice dealing with this particular client.

Rashad's care was supervised and managed by the director of the unit and the psychologist of the unit, both of whom immediately requested all of my files and any information about the family, all of which had been rejected for review by Paul Dasher. The report that was ultimately issued by the staff of Saint Clare's Hospital stated that this child had sustained such severe trauma from abuse at the hands of his father. They advised that the child should have absolutely no contact with the father ever again and that the child should be in the sole custody of his mother.[7] This advice was ignored by the courts.

The same hearing that gave custody to Child Protective Services—and ultimately the father—also removed me from any further contact with the children. I filed complaints against Judge Margaret Mary McVeigh, for having ignored and overridden the directives of the previous family court judge, who was very familiar with the case. But from then

---

7 See Appendix, Documents 6 and 7

on, my only contact with this family consisted of being periodically notified of events and issues related to the mother's distress and her treatment by the courts.

On Oct. 25th, 2005, when Rashad was twelve years old, he committed suicide.[8] But his last act of deliberate defiance against the father he hated and feared was eviscerated by the judges presiding over the case, as they allowed the father to share equal time at the boy's funeral. The court then retaliated against the mother by removing her two surviving sons to foster care. Her youngest son, born of a second marriage, was placed for adoption by DCF. The child was not even allowed to be given to his father, an artist of impeccable character and decency, who was wrongfully accused as the abuser of the children.[9]

My first-hand experience with the chicanery and backroom dealings of the organization known as the family court prompted me to begin examining this world of corruption. Ultimately it began the work of advocacy that eventually led to the nonprofit known as the Foundation for Child Victims of the Family Courts.

---

8 See Appendix, Document 8

9 Appendix Document 3 shows the note that "Shannon" sent me after her son's death.

Chapter 3

Opportunities through Loss

Behind the scenes in the early 2000s, Judge Margaret Mary McVeigh began to work on getting my license as a clinical social worker stripped from me. But in my world, my life as a therapist carried on as normal.

I had kept my client load small ever since my husband died in 1994. Ken, who had been an attorney and a CPA, had set us up with several large accounts and three homes (two in New Jersey and one in New York), so I worked only because I wanted to, not because I needed to.

But that all changed a year later. One day, my banker called while I was in the middle of a session with my client on the couch. "We have an emergency." My bank accounts were overdrawn by $65,000.

That was impossible. But it was true. The large accounts had been completely drained, and the banker told me that I had one week to pay back the $65,000.

It took a while to understand what had happened, but I learned that a bookkeeper I had hired, along with her sister, had forged hundreds of my checks over many months. They had siphoned all my money out of all my accounts, which had been linked under the advice of my attorneys and accountants managing my affairs. I had maintained a perfect credit score my whole life, but my credit score now plummeted to 250.

For the first time in years, I had to open my doors to new clients. I had never done any advertising and had never needed to solicit referrals at all. But now I needed to drum up business quickly. As soon as I began advertising, my practice rapidly expanded, and I was able to cover the $65,000 overdraft in a short period of time.

In the early 2000s evaluators were getting $100,000 to do evaluations and taking a year to do it. I charged $1500-$2500 per evaluation and produced excellent evaluations in much less time by following the standard form of fully detailed documented psychosocial diagnostic evaluations. As a result, I made enough money to recover from the devastating loss.

The bank, as per the laws of New Jersey, had changed its policies so they were no longer responsible for fraud. I had to go to the police, and I did. I took with me all the bank records and all the checks, obviously forged, hundreds of them.

But I, who had been living in this community only about ten years and had kept a low profile in private practice, was no match for the reputation of the two sisters, whose family had been in the area for generations.

The police detective told me I reminded him of someone else he had prosecuted years ago who had driven a red car like mine. He indicated that I must be trying to cover up a business failure by accusing these two sisters. He told me I was guilty of a "failure of supervision." He even questioned the circumstances surrounding my husband's death. It was outrageous.

CHAPTER 3

I went to multiple lawyers, but I was shrugged off. The response of "the police won't press charges, so there's nothing we can do" shocked me. The attorney general wasn't interested. The legal stonewalling and my lack of access to any type of intervention and criminal review were devastating. Then these two sisters used my money to hire criminal defense attorneys, threatening to sue me for defamation. It was an absolute disaster.

Criminals had preyed on me, but I was the one being treated as a criminal.

* * * * *

When I opened my doors to new clients, my professional assistance was requested by a woman who had researched my work and believed I would be able to help her in a nonprofit she wanted to develop to help facilitate the divorce process in high-conflict cases. It was called Families in Transition, FIT.

I joined her work as a pro bono independent consultant. We did monthly seminars where I spoke about high-conflict divorce, along with children's programs and work with attorneys and a hospital.

Our initial cases were mostly referred by pediatricians for family therapy as a result of very tragic circumstances. In one particular case, a seven-year-old boy was the subject of a high-conflict litigation suit that involved high-profile, extremely wealthy litigants. I was engaged as the forensic consultant to the child's mother.

In the court, I was told that I was to provide evidence related to an affidavit I had reputedly written and signed, which stated that I had interviewed the child and had come to the conclusion that the child was not the subject of sexual abuse.

However, not only had I not interviewed the child at that point, but at the time that the signed statement affidavit was presented to the court, I hadn't even been retained on the case yet. I presented evidence under oath that not only had I never written such a statement or seen the child, but the signature on the form was not mine.

However, despite the clear evidence of fraud and perjury, the judge completely disregarded my testimony and went on to transfer full custody of the child to his father.

I did move on to interview and work with the child and his extended family. I learned that, indeed, the child had been savagely abused and was suffering acutely from the physical, sexual, and emotional trauma that he had sustained for years. While there were issues related to the fitness of the child's mother, she was not an abuser of the child.

Ultimately, full custody was decided in favor of the child's maternal grandmother, which was a reasonable and beneficial outcome.

This was "the Johnny case," one of the seminal cases in building my reputation in the community and a turning point in my development of certain tactics and techniques for presenting evidence and substantiating the credibility of such evidence. But it was also one more experience that solidified my understanding of the indisputable fraud and malicious conscious intent on the part of judges to disregard the safety and welfare of children.

The founder of Families in Transition, with her charismatic personality, was an excellent spokesperson for the implementation of her non-profit as a court program.[10] As a result of her efforts and relationships, the

---

10 See Appendix Document 9

program flourished and was adopted by a family court in Sussex County, New Jersey, as a referral source. Through this, they sought to divert litigation, to resolve custody disputes accurately and constructively through mediation and arbitration, and to apply psychotherapy, in order to lead to a mutually satisfactory resolution between parties. Attorneys worked with clients on sliding-scale fees and utilized the services of FIT to assist in client relations, communication, cooperation, and dispute resolution directed in the best interests of all parties.

Through FIT, many high-conflict custody cases were successfully resolved outside of court litigation. We confronted all forms of domestic violence and child abuse, with the availability and support of police, criminal authorities, and child protective services, as well as resorting to litigation where no other alternative was available.

The acuity, expertise, and cooperation of experts from multiple disciplines, using the resources available to clients within their means, led to speedy and effective resolutions for immensely critical issues. All organizations involved in the community—the local hospital, police department, law firms, and local practitioners—all thrived.

In an article written in the *New Jersey Daily Record* in January 2002, FIT was described as a program that took the pain out of divorce. We sought to help all parties in custody litigation to equitably move through the court system and the criminal justice system in a manner that protected the integrity of the family and the rights of all parties.

Families in Transition thrived with a 98% success rate and very happy clients.

* * * * *

My private practice continued to grow as well, with physicians and schools both enthusiastic about my work, as well as the local domestic violence shelter, Strengthen our Sister, where I continued to volunteer regularly. Attorneys began referring their clients to me.

One of them was the case of a woman who was accusing her husband of domestic violence. I agreed to see both parties confidentially, write a report, and then the attorneys would decide how they wanted to use the report.

I saw the clients in person in my home office in New Jersey. The woman and her boyfriend were driven to my office by my driver. After lunch, she and I spoke in my office for 3 hours. The interview was recorded as she disclosed to me that there was no domestic violence, but that she thought he was having an affair. She indicated that her rage and jealousy caused her to accuse him of abuse.

My interview with the husband, though, showed that he was having a nervous breakdown rather than an affair. He had enjoyed a long, stable, happy marriage with his previous wife, who had died, but now he was withdrawn and severely depressed. I referred him for psychotherapy and psychopharmacology.

When I came to court as a witness and presented my report, I found that the woman had put in a complaint against me. She made the wild claim that the reason she had denied the domestic violence and admitted to her jealousy and rage was that she had been held as a hostage in my basement, bound and gagged until she agreed to tell these lies.

In response to these outrageous claims, I hired a professional photographer to make a video of the house to show that it had no basement. Also, my driver who picked up her and her boyfriend and drove them to my home office, as well as my assistant, who was present as the woman's boyfriend waited for her, bore witness to the fact that there had been no intimidation.

The refutation of her preposterous claims provided grounds to support the husband, and the divorce proceeded on equitable terms. As a result of this case, I received more referrals from that attorney and worked closely with him over time.

Another client, a middle-aged woman whose life was in the control of a conservator, was referred to me because she was charged with threatening to blow up the local courthouse. The district attorney understood there was a psychiatric component to the case. Upon review of the case, I saw that there had been considerable medical mismanagement. The client was being given medication that was acutely disrupting her mood and judgment. When I referred her to my psychopharmacological medical coverage physician in Sparta, New Jersey, to properly manage her situation, both her psychiatric and legal situations were rapidly corrected and resolved. My report to the court incorporated the medical diagnoses and assessments of the treating physician. This woman's situation was resolved and stabilized, and proper living support services were easily engaged.

The positive resolution of this case led to further referrals by other local district attorneys and attorneys in New Jersey. I also received additional referrals, of an increasingly complex nature, that other practitioners did not want to take on. These cases often involved serious criminal charges, but once the court was made aware of mitigating circumstances such as in the case above, we were able to reach a reasonable and just resolution in many of them.

I became known as a practitioner who was willing to explore difficult cases and successfully employ unique and creative interventions, and my services became more in demand.

A female police officer who was being harassed, shunned, and put in dangerous situations for being a lesbian, sought my services. Even though her performance was outstanding, she had now been suspended from the police force, and they were seeking to remove her as being psychiatrically unfit. I took on her case as she was working with her attorney to sue the police department. My work with her, my report, and my testimony on her behalf were critical in helping her be reinstated, with damages, under civil rights provisions.

One of my private practice clients was a young woman who was contemplating marriage to a man who was dominating and aggressive. Though there were concerns, she married him. As she became pregnant, his domineering and controlling behaviors increased. So did her fear, especially when he told her he knew firsthand how to dispose of bodies by burying them in freshly dug graves. The implication was that he would not hesitate to do it again.

After she married, this young woman continued seeing me intermittently. Almost two years after the birth of her daughter, Crystal, she called me to let me know her mother had walked in on the child's father straddling Crystal, naked. The police report resulted in a protective order against the father.

Little Crystal, at 22 months old, was clearly gifted, able to speak and read, able to grasp concepts of right and wrong and consider intentionality. She recounted to me that he had been doing similar activities to her for many nights when her mother thought he was reading to her and putting her to bed. When she spoke with me, Crystal repeated over and over, "Why would he do this to me?"

This was early in the days of the ascendancy of the "parental alienation" defense in family courts. This court could not conceptualize that such a small child could grapple with these issues, articulating them in thoughts and feelings and putting them into words. As a result, orders were put in place that Crystal was not to be seen in treatment and not to be engaged in any way so that no testimony could be documented. The only discussion would be legal arguments in a courtroom that had nothing to do with the child's welfare or the imminent danger and harm she faced.

The defense of this case found success only when an entire community rose up in arms to defend and protect this child. Crystal's grandmother spent tens of thousands of dollars that she did not have. But the resources were gathered and the child was rescued. By the time Crystal was 7 or 8, she was an excellent advocate and spokesman for herself, and a permanent protective order was put into place against the father, strictly limiting his contact with the child to supervised visitation.

But the division between the community and the courts was a stark one. The mental health experts and CPS all stood on the side of "parental alienation," but her teachers, medical practitioners, and family members stood on the side of the child.

It was a win, but at the cost of years of trauma and all the resources this grandmother had been able to gather over a lifetime.

*****

Over time, my work with Families in Transition came to an end, as interest in collaboration in divorce cases more and more gave way to giving full custody of the children to one parent, namely the abuser. This trend completely removed the protective parent who had raised issues of criminal culpability, as the accusations were countered by the war cry of "coaching" and "false accusations."

But my private practice work progressed as a clinician, forensic consultant, and advocate for protective parents engaged in high-conflict custody litigation. As I appeared in court with clients to observe, learn, and support them during their litigation process, my presence and activism caught the attention of public defenders, local attorneys, district attorneys, and other clients in the courtroom in my home state of New Jersey. My practice as a psychoanalyst, psychotherapist, and family therapist grew as well.

I continued my academic training. I tried to help attorneys understand the history and interpersonal dynamics within families, as well as the nature of explosive events causing the crises that brought litigants to court. And I developed unique coordination of defense techniques. As I did these things, my work evolved organically. The goal of my work and my role in each case as a clinician, family therapist, and mediator, was to attempt to elucidate a path toward conflict resolution.

At the same time, more clients were coming to me whose cases did not present a clear path to conflict resolution. The path required for child protection often involved what should have been the indictment of an abusive parent. Sometimes I saw that situations had been inaccurately and improperly diagnosed, placing vulnerable subjects in impossible situations from which they were unable to extricate themselves.

Chapter 4

Fighting My Licensure Removal

Clients of the FCVFC have often asked me if I have a personal story[11] of facing a charge of "parental alienation" in the family courts. I have told them no, the work came to me because of that first case, the case of Shannon. But I do know that I have faced corruption and collusion similar to that which has been faced by my clients. In reviewing documents as I worked on this book, I became further convinced that Margaret Mary McVeigh and Paul Dasher teamed up against me to have my LCSW-P (licensed clinical social worker psychotherapist/psychoanalyst) license removed.

In her May 29, 2001 letter to the State Board of Psychological Examiners of New Jersey, Margaret Mary McVeigh wrote,

> I am concerned that Ms. Soderman has overstepped the bounds of professional conduct and has in fact breached the basic rule of professional conduct.

---

11 See Appendix, Document 4

> *Initially, Ms. Soderman provided a 3-page report with reference to a mother and children in a Domestic Violence case with observations and recommendations, concerning a father that she had not even interviewed. The reports came directly to the Family Court without Certification or the opportunities of the parties' attorneys to properly introduce evidence.*[12]

This is a complete fraud and fabrication. She said I never saw the father, but I did see and interview him for five hours. Furthermore, if there ever was a trial, I was not informed about it and I was not present for it.

But more to the point, she said here that I provided a report, but I never made a report.[13] I never acted as an expert witness in this case. There was never even a hearing. The one who did write a report was the fraud Paul Dasher, who as of this writing has over 700 complaints lodged against him by protective parents for having destroyed their family and their children's lives.[14] He is the one who presented a report, a fraudulent one. I never did.

An attorney secured by the nonprofit Strengthen Our Sisters did eventually receive a report from me about my work on the case. A Clinical Assistant Professor at Saint Clare's Hospital also wrote a report on Shannon's son. He and I had never spoken with each other, but our reports

---

12 See Appendix, Document 1, letters from Judge Margaret Mary McVeigh.

13 When I brought a lawsuit years later, I learned in discovery that the "report" Judge Margaret Mary McVeigh referenced was the informal handwritten note I had given to Paul Dasher in the court lobby, at his request. He had blatantly lied to me about her, and she believed and acted on his lie.

14 Paul Dasher's lack of qualifications to do the work he was doing is represented in his dissertation, which can be seen at https://research.library.fordham.edu/dissertations/AAI9007176/

were completely in sync in terms of diagnosis, content, and recommendations.[15] The recommendation from that doctor was that this child should never see the father again; it would be a death knell. The court ignored him, and his prophecy came to pass.

Margaret Mary McVeigh's letter went on to say,

Then, after two (2) days of trial, on an Executive Parte basis, [Jill Jones Soderman] telephoned my secretary and left a message detailing the psychological condition of a witness including references to medications and the medical condition of the plaintiff's (her own client) attorney...[16]

I did contact Margaret Mary McVeigh's secretary, but it was not at all about the issue she described here. No, when those three attorneys accosted me in the hallway of the family court in Patterson, New Jersey, and threatened me that if I stayed on this case, I would never work in my field again, I immediately contacted the attorney general's office, and also the administration of the courts. The administration of the courts told me to contact the office of Margaret Mary McVeigh because I, as a potential witness, had been threatened.

That was the extent of my interaction with the office of Margaret Mary McVeigh. I never referred to any medications or anyone's medical condition.

During this process, I began to receive strange phone calls from individuals who seemed to be presenting themselves

---

15 See Appendix, Document 10
16 Ibid.

as potential clients requesting my services in a way that would have conflicted with my license. One woman in particular set up an appointment with me in my office, having said she was referred by another client. I thought she was peculiar but had no idea what was happening until much later. It turned out that this was an undercover agent, but I never would have known that if I had not sued those who removed my license and gone through the process of discovery.[17] The agent used the name of a client from my insurance list as a name for her referral to me.

During discovery, I learned that this undercover agent had "quoted" me as saying stupid comments I would never have said. My employment at Columbia Psychiatric Institute as the Clinical Supervisor and Adjunct Professor of Psychiatry, as well as my appointments by the Director of the Psychiatric Institute to multiple committees on human research into psychiatric medication testing, including my involvement in the DSM research projects, would militate any suggestion that I would ever engage in the commentary asserted by the attorney general's undercover agent. It must be noted that despite the cloak-and-dagger antics of this person and her partner, my engagement with her was not taped, and no attempt seems to have been made to photograph my office.

The undercover agent also claimed that I had referred my clients to a certain doctor, but that doctor was my dermatologist. The record showed that I had never referred anyone to him. This woman even described furniture in my office that did not exist. She fabricated an entire scenario, and that scenario was used against me without an

---

17 See Appendix Document 11

opportunity for me to rebut—without even my knowledge until discovery directed by me as a Pro Se client—in the course of filing multiple Federal Civil Rights actions and Civil damages lawsuits against everyone—my false accusers and my lawyers.

My clients also began to receive phone calls from the attorney general's office, whose agents had found them through their insurance filings. They were told that their relationship with me was being investigated. Some of my clients were told that agents would be coming to their homes to speak with them. Or, they were told to come to the office of the attorney general for an interview regarding their work with me. All of this was outside of any legal action. Thankfully, my clients told me what was going on, and they had enough wherewithal to refuse the agents without a warrant. None of them backed down in any way or left my practice. All were stalwart.

Agents came to my house too, standing there with clipboards wanting to come inside and see receipts of my work with my clients. I asked for their warrant, which they did not have, so I didn't allow them in. But I did mail them bills for psychotherapy services, copies of which they already had via insurance billing. I sent copies of my bills and receipts for my work, which did match up with the insurance information, to the attorney general's office. I also began to experience phone tapping. I heard a strange beeping and a hollow silence. Occasionally I answered my phone to hear a commanding anonymous voice threatening me. I even tried redialing the number via *69, but the phone disconnected.

In May of 2002, my home was the target of an arson fire that destroyed it, literally burning it to the ground.

Although I suspected that Shannon's ex-husband was involved, that was never proven. The only thing that was saved was my client records because about a month earlier an office store that was going out of business had offered to give me several large fireproof cabinets. I paid the delivery men to help me secure my client folders inside them.

But when the house was burned down, all my personal belongings were destroyed. Clothing, furniture, artwork, books, cabinets, papers, the contents of my life were destroyed. A kitten and a puppy died, and my child and I were significantly displaced. Our lives were disrupted for about a year.

I was, in fact, never able to fully reconstruct the extensive records of my years of psychoanalytic training and practice that had expanded over 37 years. It took me over a year to even begin to be able to respond to the demands of the licensing board.

As I continued to fight the licensure loss, I was undermined at every turn by court personnel, including my attorneys. One of them took my money and then abandoned me while she went off on vacations with her boyfriend. One of them took a letter I had dictated confronting the fraud and lies, and he rewrote it to be totally different. But he sent me only the last page to sign, and trustingly, I signed it. Then in court, I was shown a document that I had never seen that I had supposedly signed. This attorney completely undermined my defense. I had to fire him right in the middle of a court proceeding. Other attorneys did the same, taking my money to do whatever they wished, with complete disregard for me.

CHAPTER 4

One judge told me, "I don't care about your constitutional rights. I don't care that you are protesting. I'm going to proceed with removing your license."

Once Margaret Mary McVeigh was successful in having my license suspended in 2003, the only change I experienced was that I could no longer file for insurance claims. My practice otherwise went on as normal, since all my clients continued to work with me.

As I spoke out about the corruption in family courts, both through writing and public speaking, I became more famous, and also more infamous. I decided to go to graduate school to work on another postgraduate degree. I now know that this wasn't necessary in order to deal with the corruption, fraud, and child endangerment in family courts because they needed to be faced head-on. But at that time I was looking for a different route to deal with these problems. I was still new in the world of the family courts, and I still did not have a clear conception of what I was facing. It took ten more years to fully understand the growing plague that has overtaken this country, to destroy important institutions in order to put in place autocratic controls that generate funds through corruption and child trafficking. Going through the normal route of academia was not going to bring me closer to solving the problem, but I did not know that at the time.

In 2004 I applied and was admitted to a Master of Science in Health Sciences (MSHS) program at Touro University in New York, majoring in Law and Expert Witness Studies.

I also applied to multiple Ph.D. programs at several schools. Union Institute in Ohio was my preferred program, but I knew they accepted a very small number of students, so I applied to other programs as backups. All of them accepted me, but to my dismay, I found that during the time I was applying and being accepted, these very reputable Ph.D. programs were all losing their funding and accreditation and were no longer being offered.

When Union Institute accepted me, I was beyond thrilled. Because Union's studies were distance studies, I made plans to move to Arizona where I would spend two years studying the unique character of the Arizona court system for my dissertation. Then I planned to spend time in Texas doing the same.

Before moving to Arizona, I took all the steps to register for a license in Arizona, which included full disclosure of the 2003 license revocation in New Jersey. I sent the Arizona licensing board every document they requested, along with my long and vigorous protests of self-defense.

Once my Arizona license had been confirmed, I moved to a house in Paradise Valley that had a swimming pool, orchard, stable, and vineyard. Shortly after settling in, I flew to Ohio for the required week of orientation and first classes at Union Institute. But the classes I attended were not at all what I expected. I found the teachers to be autocratic and my fellow doctoral students to have low academic skills. On the third day, I finally learned that the program I thought I had engaged in, which was a famous and well-established independent study program, had lost its accreditation and funding, and I had been funneled into a different program without my knowledge or consent. Union Institute, it turned out, had nothing to offer me. So, I got my money back and left.

The material I had been planning for my doctoral program did not go to waste, though—I was able to use it in my MSHS program at Touro University. In contrast to the Ohio experience, my Touro University experience was an incredible one. In this program, I gained a mentor, Dr. Afshin Afrookteh, MD, who spent many hours directing my course of learning and inspiring my work.

One of the reasons I had chosen Arizona was that one of the pediatricians with whom I had worked closely, Dr. Louis Pupo in New Jersey, had referred me to a friend of his there, Dr. Louis Trunzo, who was interested in my work with children. I rented an office and opened my practice, calling it the Family Resolution Center. Doing mediation work as an advisor to the large pediatric medical practice where Dr. Trunzo practiced, I saw my clientele grow quickly.

Attorney Allison Quattrocchi, a mediator and divorce attorney, was part of a forum lecture series on high-conflict divorce, arbitration, mediation, and related topics. In the process of working on a particularly excellent lecture series that involved attorney Quattrocchi, she asked me to write a book with her, *How to Talk to Your Children About Divorce*. Some years later her company, Family Mediation Center, was awarded among the top ten most successful women-owned businesses in the country.[18]

As I collaborated with the professionals in my life, their businesses thrived as well as mine. The Family Resolution Center became an integral part of their success. Opportunities opened to them that they would not have

---

18 An article in Arizona Attorney entitled "A Building Speaks" (January 2010), states, "Allison Quattrocchi... has written and published seven succinct books on different divorce related topics. The most sought-after title is *How to Talk to Your Children About Divorce.*" The book can be seen at https://www.amazon.com/Talk-Your-Children-About-Divorce/dp/0976427168.

seen had they been unable to collaborate with a practice such as mine. They were my colleagues, but several of them were also my friends.

However, as good as my life was in Arizona, it was about to be sabotaged again. The couple from whom I rented my office decided they wanted to take over my business. She wouldn't allow a separate phone line in my office, and when the calls were routed through her, she tried to take my clients. When an Arizona magazine wanted to do an article about me and my collaborative work with the pediatricians, the woman represented herself as me and had the photo spread published without my permission using my name and identity. When she was confronted about this, she retaliated by reporting me to the Arizona licensing board, telling them to reinvestigate the licensing situation in New Jersey.

I had done all the required due diligence applications and complied with all the rules that had been requested, and the Arizona licensing board had given me an Arizona license. There was no new evidence—it was only after this false report and complaint that the board investigated.

Six to eight agents from the Arizona attorney general's office sat in a courtroom. The witnesses to my work consisted of many good individuals, including other therapists, a former judge, doctors working on controversial areas of medicine, and attorneys with whom I had collaborated.

I remember the questioning of Dr. Louis Trunzo, the pediatrician I had been working with successfully for almost a year. When he testified on my behalf, the agents questioned him as if he were the one on trial. They even threatened his license. Our very close, collegial relationship ended with Dr. Trunzo's court appearance on my behalf, though all of the patients referred to me continued to very successfully work with me. By the time I moved to New York from Arizona to begin yet another new chapter of my life, the clients, who I had quite literally rescued from disaster, were well established and flourishing in their new lives.

They did this with witness after witness who rose to speak on my behalf. With intimidation, threats, and insinuations, their licenses and their practices were threatened as if they were the ones on trial, and the judge did not stop them. I have the transcripts from this proceeding. These witnesses included medical doctors working in controversial areas of medicine with highly disturbed patients. They also included professionals who had experienced no conflicts and no issues before this day. The licensing board members were determined to bring me down.

The judge engaged in some questioning of witnesses, apparently interested in my work, but the attorney general agents even stopped the judge from asking his questions.

I had two completely useless attorneys. They fully understood that my rights were being violated, but their advice was to cooperate and be humble. Though the documentation was clearly there, I was never allowed to present the evidence of my innocence. My license was stripped for the second time.

It was about this time that I received word that Shannon's son had committed suicide. I was devastated.

I decided that litigation of past events that I did not, at the time, even begin to understand, much less be prepared to comprehend, might have directed me to protect, organize, and document evidence. I did not understand that every lie could be addressed and litigated. I did not understand at the time that statements such as, "I do not care about your Constitutional rights," accompanied by factually incorrect statements, were able to be presented as documented evidence; never submitted by my two attorneys were statements that would have resulted in a successful appeal of the kangaroo court trial to which I was subject, as the long arm of the New Jersey court Judge Mary Margaret McVeigh reached out to Arizona, to the director of the Arizona licensing board, as was clear in a retrospective reading of my own court transcripts.

My failure to address the malevolent fraud committed against me by the Arizona licensing board, as well as the vicious, malevolent character assassination to which I was subject through the collusion of official court actors, has haunted me as I have been drawn into confronting fraud and criminal coverups committed by the Arizona licensing board over successive years. As recently as 2021, the Arizona board members lied on record regarding complaints filed against a specific PsyD evaluator who was reported to have been subtly, but obviously, masturbating in front of a fifteen-year-old boy while in "treatment" sessions with him. Detailed written complaints were sent to the licensing board, accompanied by police reports. Referenced in my written complaints were the subject of testimony by board officials who overtly and concretely lied about my written statements.

My written statements, on behalf of my client and his son, were redacted from the record. The attorney for the client's abuser/subject under investigation also lied in testimony before the Arizona licensing board, even

CHAPTER 4

though all of my communications with the attorney were in writing. At the administrative law hearing, the written communications were not admitted, yet the oral hearsay statements admitted as arguments on behalf of an entirely incompetent, debauched individual were allowed into evidence to which I was never able to respond, though I was present by phone at the administrative hearing.

The PsyD evaluator who is the subject of this particular commentary has been the subject of numerous social media complaints that support the experience of the client and his son, who did evade contact with this predator. The court that admitted this individual's report did eventually dismiss the report. The court related that this practitioner would not be allowed to engage in practice before this court in the future. The members of the Arizona licensing board, in collusion with the attorney for the depraved, deceitful, destructive PsyD evaluator, overturned this practitioner's license suspension, thus returning a depraved predator to an ability to prey on innocent children and vulnerable protective parents.

As of 2022, it was my understanding that this corrupt individual and his partners in crime joined together to create a practice of "reunification" services. This is another feature of the cottage industry for which Richard Gardner, MD, author of the depraved concept of "parental alienation" laid the groundwork. "Reunification services" have become another feature of the current expansion of the cottage industry generated by Gardner. These collaborators are "trained" like dowsers, seeking out parent "alienators" and then deploying their reunification interventions to re-educate the parent to "unsee" what they have seen. In this way the plan to reorient parental communications with their children. As a result, the children will become thoroughly confused and disoriented/detached from their own sensory and intuitive messages that what is being done to them is painful, frightening and against their will.

On the advice of a friend, I moved to Nyack, New York, and began work on developing the nonprofit that became the Foundation for Child Victims of the Family Courts.

* * * * *

Over the ten years of transition, even as I moved from New Jersey to Arizona, then to New York and back to New Jersey, I continued working on fighting the unjust licensure removal. I appealed this ruling; then, with the help of a competent attorney, I sued Margaret Mary McVeigh and Paul Dasher. I sued the licensing board, sued my attorneys, and filed complaints against the judges who were hearing the case.

As Margaret Mary McVeigh moved from family court to probate court, I continued to write about her court corruption.[19] People began to contact me because of my writings against her. One woman gave permission to release all her information to help others. She said that Margaret Mary McVeigh had ravaged her in probate court and left her life in shambles.[20] She was only one of many whose lives Margaret Mary McVeigh destroyed.

Over time, clients began to come to me trembling, shaking with fear, telling me that Judge Margaret Mary McVeigh had said if she found out they were even reading my articles, she would send them to jail.

In 2008 I received my MSHS from Touro. This is the same year the FCVFC became a nonprofit. It had

---

19 See Appendix Document 12
20 See Appendix Document 13

exploded as an epiphany for the direction that my life needed to take from this point on. By that point, I was convinced that there were no further areas of education or training that addressed the real-life problems of fraud, collusion, and pure corruption in family courts across the country.

In 2011, after ten years of fighting, I finally withdrew from pursuing justice regarding my licensure. I could spend another ten years fighting my own battles. Or I could focus more completely on doing something constructive for others. I made my choice. All I wanted then, and now, has been to continue to build this model organization that confronts the lies and larceny of lawyers and the family courts who act in collusion, complicit with protecting their own. I was going to turn my attention fully to focus on building up my nonprofit, the Foundation for Child Victims of the Family Courts.

Chapter 5

A Yellow Ribbon for H

In 2004, the book *How to Talk to Your Children About Divorce* was published, which I had co-written with attorney Allison Quattrocchi. In 2005, I had a book signing in New York, where several experts would be present, including a pediatrician who would be talking about the impact of trauma on children.

A group of parents from another state organized a busload of people to come to it. One of those was a woman carrying cards that said, "A Yellow Ribbon for H," with her son's name. She told me that she was recently back from the military, where she was a pilot of the largest cargo planes during the war in Kuwait. She was very skilled and decorated for her service. She was now in the reserves, and her child was around 3 years old and in preschool. He had been in the care of his father and his father's sister while she was gone.

When she returned and first saw her child, "H" grabbed at her to try to pull her shirt down and grab her breasts. He also tried to position himself to put his penis in her mouth, gyrating and masturbating. She was horrified. She took him to the pediatrician and received confirmation of abuse, but then very quickly she found that a protective order had been placed against her. She landed in court and was ordered not to see her child except under supervised visitation, and that only if she admitted that she was making it all up. She did not comply and was then blocked from seeing her child.

Yet the child was still having such extreme behavior problems in school that he was removed from the preschool program. He was pulling down little girls' pants and behaving in inappropriate aggressive ways.

"H" was about three and a half when this started. He was about five when I heard his mother's story. Her cards, "A Yellow Ribbon for H," signaled that her son was a prisoner of war and she was advocating for his return.[21]

She had not been allowed to see "H" at all in all this time. When she asked my advice about whether she should finally agree to cooperate with the court, I said, "Absolutely not. You have to fight this." She showed me the reports from both the school and the pediatrician. "This is unacceptable. You should not cooperate," I said.

My last communication with this mother was after she returned to her home state. She sent me an email telling me she had decided to try to work with the court and get supervised visitation.

Fourteen years later, in 2019, when I was in Albany, New York, to speak at the Battered Mothers' Custody Conference, I heard a woman calling my name. I turned to see someone that I vaguely remembered who was tall, thin, and very pale. She carried with her a tiny dog, her emotional support dog.

---

21 See Appendix Document 14

CHAPTER 5

"Do you remember me?" she asked. "I was at your book signing in Nyack."

When she said that, I did remember. I said, "A yellow ribbon for H."

"I should have listened to you and tried to fight for him," she said. "But I never saw him again. When I went to court, I lost all custody and all contact with him." She was not even allowed to have any knowledge of his whereabouts.

She never had any other children. But now, every year, she came to the Battered Mothers' Custody Conference to support other mothers like herself.

PART TWO

The First Few Years of the FCVFC

Chapter 6

The Early Days of the Foundation

As of February 2008, the Foundation for Child Victims of the Family Courts was recognized as a 501(c)3 nonprofit, to help children stay with their protective parents. We have been dedicated to advancing the cause of child protection through research, education, publishing, and speaking about what we've learned as the result of our work throughout the United States. We analyze and evaluate cases, intervening and advocating for those who do not know what they stepped into when they stepped into the family courts.

The work that became the Foundation for Child Victims of the Family Courts began in seed form in 1999 with Shannon's case. It was a response to what I told myself was a unique situation, as at the time, I could not imagine the plethora of cases similar in nature. And yet, more similar cases began coming to me over the years. And again, I saw the suffering of children and their families, as well as the emotional distance, apathy, and dismissiveness of the professionals associated with litigating these cases.

Rather than being weighed down with despair, I was spirited to explore areas of public health administration, law, and services, as well as the work of psychiatric forensic experts. This combination seemed to hold the keys to understanding a path forward to gain a grip on this problem.

Apart from extensive writing about parental alienation, I could find no literature related to court corruption and the undermining of the legal process that allowed for children's lives to be destroyed.

As my work began, I was supported by the interest and enthusiasm of many pediatricians in the areas of New York and New Jersey. Because they referred child clients to me, I was able to engage with families seeking to protect their children.

For the most part in these early days, my assistants and I operated without an attorney, both because of a lack of resources and because of the difficulty of finding attorneys who agreed with my way of doing things. I worked with paralegals to figure out the laws, write motions, and file documents pro se. We learned step by step the procedural issues for each case. We tried to understand what had happened in the family and with each family member. We inquired about what events led to the current crisis threatening the family, and what had legally transpired in the case. Then we could define our goals and plan strategies to achieve those goals.

An early case, referred to me by a pediatrician, involved a woman who died from an accidental drug overdose. This was a young mother whose husband had brutally beaten her in front of her two little children, as an object lesson for them. She and her two children were now living with her parents; she was acutely depressed and in despair.

CHAPTER 6

Her psychiatrist, the head of psychiatric services at Newton Memorial Hospital, refused to see clients who were late to an appointment. To have their prescriptions renewed, they would have to take the next appointment, which could be weeks or months away.

This doctor, knowing the level of trauma and suffering this woman had experienced, deprived her of a desperately needed antidepressant. She went to the home of a drug dealer, and in a desperate attempt to overcome her despair, she overdosed on those drugs.

The maternal grandmother now became the primary custodian of the two young children. But the biological father, who had played a large role in his ex-wife's death, wanted them.

In this case, I prevailed in court to keep the children with their grandmother. One of the little children, quite verbal and intelligent, described how the father had beaten up his mother, hitting her repeatedly.

I advocated for the grandparents to be able to keep the children, to get resources to stabilize their homes and families and to have better lives for the kids.

In this instance, the court was very helpful. We were able to maintain supervision of this family and this case, not even needing to work with Child Protective Services.

Once the children were safe in the custody of the grandparents, I provided psychotherapy for the entire family through the services of the Foundation for a good 7 or 8 years. This included aunts and uncles and their children. They became my core private practice, all with serious medical and psychiatric issues, as well as family dysfunction due to generational trauma.

The demonstrable success of working with these individuals was a win that was understood by the medical practitioners around them. As a result, we became a source of help for others in the community, both in their psychiatric needs and in court interventions. For example, I explained to the court how the psychodynamics of the family and interpersonal issues required help and structure that would best be afforded by a certain member having custody.

These interactions increased both our credibility and our practice.

The pediatricians who referred cases to me became the core of my collaborators in eventually building the Foundation for Child Victims of the Family Courts, as well as the Foundation's original board members. Others enthusiastically came together as well, including childcare workers, people in the medical field, and social workers, to assist in developing the structure and framework of the Foundation. They received no financial compensation and no remuneration other than the satisfaction of being engaged in a project they considered worthwhile.

Local interest and support generated referrals and interest of prospective clients who were suffering with impossible cases related to children being seized through Child Protective Services and dragged into foster care and adoption, as families stood helplessly on the sidelines unable to protect their children.

Clients became test subjects for our evolving work and methods, which grew out of my diagnostic skills as a clinician. These were then applied to the broader problem of addressing the court system, mostly without the assistance of attorneys. It seemed that attorneys generally felt that the work of the Foundation was too controversial and confrontational for them to want to have any public presence. Though there were some whose interest was piqued by the ethical issues plus the intellectual challenge of actually defending clients and working for their best interest. Those individuals were willing to be hired under the condition of never revealing their presence as professionals in our work, and being paid in cash for their services, leaving no paper trail to identify them.

But these attorneys helped us see what was going on with the failure of the court system, as well as sketching out a roadmap to see procedural processes, whereby we could begin to intervene. The services of paralegals became incredibly important and helpful to us, since paralegals were not in jeopardy of losing their licenses, as they were working confidentially and on an intellectual intervention basis.

As we took on cases that had outstanding moral and legal value, and as we began to be able to define the nature of violations that had clear access to intervention, we persisted with confronting palpably identifiable constitutional violations in the family court.

* * * * *

In one case, a mother's eight-month-old baby had slid off his sister's lap and bumped his head. They put a compress on and gave him some pain reliever. When out of an abundance of caution they took the child to the doctor, Child Protective Services was alerted and opened an investigation, even though the child had no physical injuries other than the bump on the head. The events that followed led to years of aggressive legal intervention and the seizure of the child into foster care with attempts to have him adopted out.

The father, from Jamaica, had a doctorate in ministry. The mother was a real estate agent who owned many properties in Queens. They were upper middle class and prosperous. When I was contacted as a consultant, court dates were being set, with a very nasty judge.

At one of the hearings, the 80-year-old grandmother of the little boy accompanied us, very elegant in her hat and gloves. As we sat together in the pew waiting for court to begin, the mother closed her eyes and prayed silently. The judge came in, glared at her, and went to the bench to go through the roll call. When this case was called, the judge contacted the bailiff and read the charges that referred the case for a full CPS investigation.

Then the judge ordered the bailiff to arrest the mother for praying in court—because of the separation of church and state, according to that judge. She was taken away in handcuffs and shackles.

She had been a pro se client, but we were able to find a helpful attorney in the areas of family and criminal law. We went on to prosecute, and win, a First Amendment case. This mother sued for damages and settled for $360,000.

"Use that money to sue CPS," I urged her. "Don't cooperate with them." They were trying to take her son away for no reason. They had tried to use the arrest for praying in court to paint her as psychotic and unfit. But her attorneys urged her to cooperate, to comply, to play nice. She listened to them instead of listening to me. So since she decided to pursue a different strategy, I left her case. After protracted, horrendous court filings back and forth, she lost custody. Her son became trapped in foster care. When she was finally able to locate him after he turned 18, he was entrenched with his foster care family and didn't want to engage with her.

CHAPTER 6

This began our fight with "Mercy First," a multi-million-dollar megalithic "nonprofit" that takes care of the whole package: foster care, adoption placement, and group home care. Medical and psychiatric services for the children are also taken care of in-house.

This was the organization that CPS worked with to take this child away from his biological family. I wrote articles about how there is no mercy with "Mercy First." The Foundation, in its earliest days, began to receive significant attention.

* * * * *

In 2011, while I was still on a steep learning curve about the corruption in the family court system, I was contacted by a woman who asked to retain my services as a consultant to her attorney. Because I was retained by the attorney rather than the litigant, I was bound to confidentiality and client contact by the framework the attorney provided.

But the attorney was completely incompetent. She appeared to be invested in being a therapist to her client, presenting herself as a nurturing figure rather than one set to fight for the truth in court.

This mother, a respected medical professional, had three children who were being horrendously physically neglected and sexually abused by the father. The father's interactions with the public showed him to be a bizarre character, idiosyncratic, and extremely aggressive.

The children were involved with the father's sexual preoccupations. All three were acutely suicidal. The youngest, at seven years old, ruminated about ways to kill himself. He had even gone to the highest point in the house and was poised to jump off when the mother convinced him to come back. One action he took to protect himself from his father was to smear feces all over his body, devolving into functional psychosis.

The father came from a very wealthy family. In court, it was revealed that the retainer for his attorney was $250,000. That went to pay off an evaluator who was so comfortable in her bias against the mother that there was no need for pretense in her report. It was nakedly and unadulteratedly a hit job against the mother.

The mother's attorney challenged nothing, but left these extremely biased and nakedly twisted and unethical reports in place. She lost every single potential advantage that she should have won.

I had connected the attorney with an expert, a highly credible and famous forensic psychiatrist. This expert was theoretically retained by the attorney, and he wrote a report related to the ancestral history of schizophrenia and incest that was known to exist through generations of the father's family, potentially diagnosing the father as suffering from a deteriorating schizophrenic process. But not only was the expert never paid, but also the attorney never presented the expert's report in court.

I spent a full week in court, days full of testimony and court activity. But though I was present at the court, my advice was ignored, and I was constrained by the terms of my engagement with the attorney. There was absolutely nothing I could do to offer the litigant advice or direction.

The psychiatric evaluator's report was a major reason the mother lost her professional licensures. She was never again able to work in her profession. In addition, she lost custody of her children and possession of her house with its contents. The courts ordered the house to be transferred to the father so that he could occupy the house with the children. She was left virtually homeless, and her parents, who had attempted to support her legal fees, were practically bankrupt.

If I had not been engaged by this mother's attorney, I would have been filing complaints against this attorney's license. But as things stood, my hands were tied. As a result of that experience, I never again allowed myself to be retained by an attorney in that manner.

This client, who never did really become my client, received advice from another survivor of high-conflict custody litigation. It read:

> *I'm sorry you are going through a custody battle with your ex-husband. I see you filed a motion to disqualify. Stop all that if you want to see your kids. If I were you, I would go to the court, smile, show remorse for your reactions, and get yourself into therapy. Getting angry and attacking a judge is not going to get you anywhere. If one judge is disqualified, you will get another.*
>
> *My ex claimed in an ex parte motion that there was an Amber Alert being processed on my son when there was no Amber Alert and he knew where I was at all times.*
>
> *After his attorney achieved multiple continuances of the return date, they amended their plan to use my emotional response against me. Of course I went through the usual emotional shock, outrage, feelings against the system, and screams, which delayed my custodial rights for 11 months.*

To regain custody, I learned to accept that domestic violence and lies are tolerated and often used as a custody strategy to destabilize a mom. Moms are not respected in American culture. Dads can be marginal parents, but a mom has to be perfect.

Discrimination against women in America is real. I studied black culture to learn how they survived discrimination to come out on top in the long haul. They smile and tolerate and never behave like that angry, crazy mom.

I did rebuild, regain custody, built a business, served as room mom for my son's class for the past 4 years and am returning to court for decision making with family relations recommendations to support me.

I never react in public and always smile. If I feel uncomfortable in a room I pick up a tray and start serving people. I never ask for anything. I don't receive child support and alimony. I give and I don't get back. I only draw the line when my ex tries to sleep in my tent while camping. I have self-respect.

* * * * *

The protocols that would become central to the work of the Foundation developed slowly with trial and error. As of this time, they are solidified with unyielding conviction, based on results that have laid the path for how the Foundation now operates.

Chapter 7

The Fog in Puyallup

One Friday night at 9 pm in 2014, I received a phone call. "I'm going to die within 48 hours if I don't get help," the young female voice said. Then she hung up the phone.

I dialed *69, and a woman answered. I explained who I was and what had just happened. We undertook a rapid review and assessment to direct our next actions.

I learned that this 15-year-old girl, in the primary custody of her father, had been starving herself for months. Child Protective Services, the family courts, and the family doctor were all ignoring her plight.

When the mother had brought to the authorities' attention allegations against her husband of the sexual abuse and child endangerment of her two daughters, then the protective parent, the mother, became guilty of the familiar accusation of "parental alienation." The mother was aware of no further steps she could take. If she had not responded to a stranger over the phone, I am convinced that the 15-year-old girl who found me online and called me would have died.

Upon information and belief that the child's life was in danger, I recommended that the mother take her to a hospital in a different jurisdiction, a different community, which she did. I recommended that the hospital physician contact the state attorney general's office, in order to bypass Child Protective Services, who had not done their job. I was going to be in touch with the attorney general's office too. The hospital doctor corroborated her medical status, and the attorney general's office undertook criminal intervention.

This adolescent girl and her sister had been enduring sexual abuse at the hands of their father and stepbrother. The sister had chosen the path of least resistance, to engage sexually with her father and stepbrother; that was isolating this young girl further, causing her to feel even more hopeless. She had determined that her only option if she didn't get help was to waste away and die.

As I was sent photos of this girl, I saw her emaciation. She had been fainting, even in school, which was a sign of malnutrition. But the family doctor said she was fine.

During the investigation, I was able to obtain records through the Freedom Of Information Act (FOIA). The records from the medical board included the complete disciplinary record of this particular family doctor. The records included information about his personal psychiatric status of depression, drug abuse, and suicidality, along with multiple complaints from his patients. With records like these, he had moved his practice many times. He had been given a special dispensation to practice in the rural area where this girl's father and family members lived, because this rural area of Puyallup, Washington, required a doctor.

The medical records from this physician indicated that the 15-year-old girl's weight was slim but within a normal weight range. It was only upon talking with her that I learned, not only was she weighed with her coat on, but she put rocks in her pockets.

One of the unique factors of this case involved my access to the children's father. I met with him confidentially via video to discuss his daughter's medical condition, as well as my recommendations to the attorney general for custody transfer and termination of his parental rights. This father was unique in that he openly defended his position that men should be able to have sexual contact with their children, basing this position on the teachings of Richard Gardner, MD. This father expressed to me his belief that the current social environment in our country was repressive and unhealthy. He felt angry at his ex-wife for sexual inhibitions regarding his espousal of a different sexual ethic and her position concerning the children.

As a result of these confidential communications, we were able to work out an expedited transfer. At the criminal court hearing, at which I was present and allowed to speak, the attorney general told the father that if he offered any opposition to the transfer, then she would prosecute him to the full extent of the law, for sexual assault and child sexual abuse.

By the direction of this attorney general, the case moved swiftly through Child Protective Services. But family court proceedings were more complex. As they often do, the family courts attempted to undermine the criminal court proceedings. The family court judge labeled the child with the life-threatening medical condition as simply a spoiled brat who just wanted to be with her mother. Even though the father was financially well off, this family court judge penalized the mother for the loss of child support. This judge also took 16 out of 32 pages of transcript to berate me because of my quick intervention in the case. She supported the recommendations of the guardian ad litem, a former military attorney and great supporter of the father. Despite the clear medical recommendations, this judge expressed an opinion that the directives to transfer the child were inappropriate and recommended continued contact with the father.

Despite this, and with the strong support of the attorney general, the custody transfer took place less than a week after the hearing. While the mother was being cleared of a false diagnosis of Munchhausen by Proxy, the girl was placed with other relatives who welcomed her.

Just days before receiving the call from this girl, I had been working on another case with Eric Mart, the current expert in diagnosing and evaluating Munchhausen by Proxy. I asked him about this case in Puyallup, and he was willing to take on the case. Our client, this protective mother, flew to New Hampshire to be evaluated by Dr. Mart and cleared of this diagnosis. She was.

The family court judge was given no choice in the matter. Everything was successful, and the child was transferred into the custody of her mother. As time passed, the family forwarded me a steady array of photos. I learned that within one month this girl had gained 22 pounds and was now out of the danger zone that would have led to heart failure or death. She was enrolled in a new high school, learning to drive, and attending her first high school prom.

The pictures of this beaming beautiful girl remain in my collection of rescued children.

There are many more memorable stories, but the theme that runs through them is this: at every step, at every turn, these cases consist of hand-to-hand combat with the family court system. Without the dedication of the protective parent working in cooperation with the Foundation, these positive outcomes would not have come about.

Chapter 8

Sisters in Crisis

When 81-year-old Milton Cletus Fabre was found guilty of murder and sentenced to prison, the judge said, "I think everyone in this courtroom today has been shocked by what they heard." He was referring to the testimony given by Tracy Fabre, Milton's surviving daughter, and one of her brothers. The murder victim was Tracy's 49-year-old sister, Tamara.

The judge added, "I believe every word they said."[22] These words were the first affirmation Tracy had ever heard of the horror she and her siblings had experienced.

In 2016, I was privileged to participate in a podcast interview with Tracy Fabre. Tracy told us the fifty-year backstory to the account of her sister's murder.[23] She talked about growing up with this extremely abusive and dangerous man, and how she and her sister were bonded over the terror of their father. They were allowed only one meal per day, so

---

22 Alexis, Krell, "Adult children vilify their father at sentencing for fatally stabbing their sister," *The [Tacoma] News Tribune*, June 26, 2016. https://www.thenewstribune.com/news/local/crime/article85907092.html

23 You can listen to the whole interview at "Stop Child Abuse Now (SCAN)—1489," *Blog Talk Radio*, November 17, 2016. https://www.blogtalkradio.com/naasca/2016/11/18/stop-child-abuse-now-scan--1489.

they went to bed hungry almost every night. Looking back at the pictures, Tracy saw that Tamara's starvation was obvious. Her eyes were hollow and deep-set, her skin sallow. How did school authorities not recognize it? How did the community not know? One teacher did try to get help because Tamara was fainting in school from her starvation. But Mr. and Mrs. Fabre claimed she was just seeking attention.

Always dirty and unkempt, the girls were bullied at school because of lice and bad smells. Tracy bullied other kids too. Later on in life, she recognized her bullying actions as trauma play, simply acting out what she was experiencing at home. Tracy said,

> *When my dad would get upset, he would roll his tongue between his teeth and start breathing heavily through his nose. His eyes would get big and wild, and we would know, we'd better run. That was our cue that my dad was going to start hitting people. [Forty years later] Tamara said, "Tracy, I was like a little wilted flower. I would run and I'd hide. I was so scared. Then, I would watch from my hiding spot, you being beaten. I would watch Dad hitting you and beating you. And I wanted to protect my baby sister, but I couldn't."*

Every time we would say something, we were always wrong... I was constantly being called a liar. I questioned my own reality a lot of times.[24]

If anyone contradicted the abusive dad, he grabbed a weapon. Tracy told about a time he grabbed a huge candlestick, raised it above his head, and yelled for the

---

24 Ibid.

CHAPTER 8

offending party to get down on their knees and beg for his forgiveness. "I'm going to bash your head off the wall, and I'm going to kill you."[25]

They saw it happen. He got angry at the cocker spaniel and stomped that little dog to death in front of his children. When Tracy was 12 years old, she broke a pencil. Her father beat her with a two-by-four and nearly killed her. These were harbingers of what was to come.

The father respected no boundaries. "I remember him going outside to look through the bedroom windows while Tamara and I would be getting dressed. I remember trying to cover up because he was outside looking in, and he got angry about that and he said, "Well, you should be able to get dressed in front of your father because if your windows open, the neighbors can see you and I should be able to see you first." It is no surprise that a man like this called his daughters the "c" word and the "b" word.

These children never should have had to be in a position to speak up for themselves. The evidence was there, but the community failed them. While Tracy suffered from anorexia her whole life, Tamara became an alcoholic. Tamara left home in 1984 but returned in 2015 to care for her mother who was dying of lung cancer. The dad wouldn't care for her at all. He despised her.

Before she died, the mom made Tamara promise to stay to take care of the dad. She agreeddid, but only a few months later she was dead. Tracy was the only one of the seven siblings willing to speak up about what happened that night. She and lay full blame at the feet of the 81-year-old abuser.

---

25 Ibid.

The murder of Tamara did not start with any sort of "elder abuse" on her part—it was a culmination of Milton's 50 years of abuse and control. Milton had no injuries, while Tamara had 17 stab wounds and her throat was slit. He was saturated in her blood while she lay dying. Then he got up and washed his hands, just as he had done when he beat Tracy when she was 12 years old.

For 48 years Tracy had protected the secret, not knowing who, if anyone, she could trust. But she obtained her master's degree in clinical social work, to help women and children from severely traumatized households. She started advocacy work to fight for kids. She has spoken about the abuse she and her sister endured. Because it needs to be known that it is only the criminals who are served by silence and secrecy.

* * * * *

In another notorious case, a mother contacted me in 2017, sending an enormous amount of documentation related to the court process and her personal history. Her ex-husband was accused of physical, sexual, and emotional cruelty in the course of her marriage. But the accounts provided by the children's mother and by the children were disregarded in family court. The mother was accused of "parental alienation" and "coaching," and the children were isolated in his custody.

The chronicles of the court records indicate a pattern of hair-splitting, dismissive denial of the children's claims, minimization of complaints, and parsing words on legal technicalities that continuously missed the point of the children's suffering. Thus, the children were forced to live for years in a state of fear through threats of physical, sexual, and emotional violence and deprivation as they were consigned to the isolation from their mother in the custody of a father whom they had fled.

The father remarried and became the father of another child whose abuse and suffering presented as additional torture to the other siblings. They were kept from providing any form of intervention or comfort to their baby half-sister and their abused new stepmother.

My work with the three girls and their mother revolved around developing a diagnostic profile of an individual who I categorized with a diagnosis of pseudo psychopathic schizophrenia, which involved a complex layering of personality traits that moved through areas of labile mood, labile reality testing, acute paranoia, grandiosity, and a psychotic level of thought process that involved conviction as to his spiritual superiority, ascendancy, and connection to God, which seemed to be embraced by the community despite what should have been apparent to onlookers as to the clear fear and suffering of his progeny.

We worked with a skilled and talented local attorney who came out of retirement to work on the case, knowing the character and immense harm these children had suffered in the course of their lives and the level of abuse they experienced at the hands of a court system that was indifferent to their words and chronicling of their horrifying experiences with their father.

My work with the attorney and the attorney general's office was facilitated by the girls' empowerment to express and articulate their day-to-day interactions and the trials and tribulations of their existence. These were then developed as legal arguments, finally making it clear to the attorney general's office that these children had been placed in the custody of a dangerous individual who never should have been allowed to have any parenting advantages over these children at any point in their lives.

The attorney general hated me and acted contemptuously toward me, but he acknowledged the truth of the case. The last of the daughters who was still underage was released from the custody of this alleged abuser in 2018.

* * * * *

There are many, many accounts of children pleading for help. Will we listen? The answer so far has been a resounding "no" as horror stories related by advocates, experts, parents, and children themselves produce no meaningful action on behalf of children, ages birth to eighteen.

While there are rumblings, heads bobbing and lips moving in some quarters, the facts are that children's lives across the United States continue to face dangers through multiple forms of exploitation via abuse, neglect, and sheer abject indifference to the infliction of suffering by unfit custodians.

PART THREE

Background of the "Parental Alienation" Accusation in Family Court

Chapter 9

Reports of Child Sexual Abuse, with Historical Context

When a child experiences inappropriate sexual interaction, we now know incontrovertibly from an abundance of evidence that this interaction is traumatizing to the child's psyche, whether this interaction takes the form of direct, obvious sexual contact or whether it is exposure to sexual behavior. (Such behaviors can include viewing the adult masturbating, being shown sexually explicit material, an adult voyeuristically watching the child bathe, go to the bathroom, or dress.)

Whether the inappropriate behavior is subtle, has not incurred obvious pain or visible injury, or even if the behavior has seemed pleasurable to the child and has not caused immediate fear or concern, the assessment of sexual contact or direction to engage in behavior that causes the child to speak to a parent must be taken seriously and explored fully.

It may come as a surprise to learn that only in relatively recent years in our world's history has even stranger abuse been designated as a criminal activity. Society's ambivalent relationship with child sexual abuse needs to be pulled out from the shadows and examined.

Incidents of incest are under-reported because incest has been and continues to be a crime of access, power, and shame. Given the under-reporting of incest and all forms of family sexual abuse, the magnitude of the crimes must be viewed with grave concern for the seriousness and impact that has motivated the protective parent and child subjects who seek protection against an abuser.

The crimes of incest have historically been broadly treated with denial, dissociation, or jokes that hide the real covert approval of incest. The crude joke that a man rejects his prospective virgin wife because any girl who is not good enough for her father, brothers, and uncles is certainly not good enough for him, imparts the obvious implication of power over girls and women. Such power is amplified in the crude joke that a virgin is defined as a girl who can run faster than her father, brother, or uncles. Jokes that misrepresent impregnation, suggesting that a female cannot become pregnant on the first penile contact may be humorous but certainly reflect a cultural bias toward male infliction of power and authority in inducing female compliance with sexual demand by dismissing concern over consequences of actions. The theme of consequences to actions will be a refrain throughout the writings moving forward as consequences to the present and future of a democratic society heavily rest on protecting our children and not creating a culture of ignorant, psychopathic survivors of abuse and corruption who then continue the legacy of ever greater abuse and corruption.

Psychiatry has explored childhood depression, schizophrenia, ADD, ADHD, and disorders related to biology, but from its onset in the Victorian age, psychoanalysis came face to face with incest and childhood sexual abuse, delivering results as per subjects' liberation from forbidden memories.

Father of the field of psychoanalytic study, Sigmund Freud, addressed sexual aberration and the destructive lifelong consequences in his original treatment explorations. Freud's initial treatment population consisted of women who experienced incest and who, in speaking of their early childhood traumas, recovered from the symptoms that were destroying their adult lives. Women who were catatonic came to life and were restored to functioning. Freud understood the connection between sexual assault trauma and the "wandering womb" designations now known to be the sequelae of a traumatic assault.

The hostility Freud experienced from his truthful observations and the clear criminal connections associated with male heads of household caused him to pull back from his original theses and rediscover the wheel in the form of transforming life as experienced into life as removed into the world of fantasy. Sigmund Freud maintained his medical license to practice yet most probably at the same time deepened his pessimism about the nature of man and society as referenced in *Civilization and Its Discontents* and other writings related to man's failure to control instincts of sex and aggression. Freud also most probably delayed social enlightenment indefinitely as we continue as a society to struggle with defining the limits of sexual and aggressive incursions justifying overpowering force to suffocate the intelligence that makes demands beyond seizing the moment.

The truth was shut down, replaced by what would become the hallmark of psychiatry, the failure to distinguish between fact and fantasy or to understand the nuggets of truth within the fantasy that uncovered the facts. Richard Gardner, MD, forensic psychiatrist and author of the concept he marketed (parental alienation) played fast and loose with the psychoanalytic fascination with thought and memory. Gardner negated fact and science as he created a theory of sexual functioning and biology as related to children that did not and does not exist.

The so-called facts advanced by Richard Gardner never existed in science and biology but served only to create a legal argument seized by lawyers to create a pathway to plausible doubt and a "treatment intervention" that manipulates children's experience of their own bodily reality suggesting that what they feel and experience is based on the attitudes taught to them by their parents, for the parent's own selfish reasons. The projections of a warped, self-serving, manipulating mind geared toward forcing children into sexual contact with adults and seeking to hijack the part of the population that has not as yet succumbed to abject lies is fully based on the infantile urge to overcome prohibition against the fulfillment of infantile wishes for any form of gratification imagined by an adult psyche that lacks compassion, judgment, and foresight.

It would be years before dissociation was recognized as a critical element of trauma. Revelations of sexual assault became "fantasies" and "wishes," and later, "lies." Those who enabled the suppression of early childhood trauma became psychiatrists and court-appointed evaluators and experts in family courts across the country.

This is one of the seeds that was planted to eventually allow children to be transferred from the hands of their protective parents into the hands of abusers.

Chapter 10

Richard Gardner, the Father of "Parental Alienation Syndrome," in His Own Words

The field of reunification therapy is based on the theories promoted by Richard Gardner, MD. But contrary to all that is known medically and scientifically and psychiatrically as to the trauma sexual activity causes to children, Richard Gardner advocates and normalizes sexual activity between adults and children.

Gardner's work has set the stage for the development of a society without norms or morals, as is being accomplished through the family court system. Following his lead, they are producing a criminal population of murderers and child abusers.

Gardner promoted his fantasies and theories on childhood sexuality through his own private publishing company, Creative Therapeutics. Through his books, cassettes, and videotapes, he marketed himself as a forensic psychiatrist, claiming that he had testified as an expert in approximately 400 cases, both criminal and civil, in

25 states.[26] He advertised himself as advocating for the defense in child sexual abuse cases.

Promoting child sexual abuse for the survival of the species

Gardner bases his promotion of sexual activity in the child on an ostensible desire to keep the human species going. As such, he calls the child a "survival machine." He uses the term "charged-up child" as a potential progenitor likely to transmit their genes through the birth process at an early age. Gardner postulates that when a child is drawn into sexual encounters at an early age, the child is likely to become highly sexualized and will crave sexual experiences during the pre-puberty years. The younger the "survival machine" is at the time sexual urges appear, he says, the longer will be the span of procreative activity and the greater the likelihood the individual will create more "survival machines" in the next generation.[27]

Gardner specifically advocated for the procreative purposes of the white race. His absorption and support of the Nazi theory of eugenics is a thread that filters through his work.[28]

There is an evolutionary benefit to sexual practices known as paraphilias, according to Gardner. He advocates many different types of human sexual behavior such as

---

26 Richard Gardner, "Qualifications of Richard A. Gardner, M.D. for Providing Court Testimony," http://richardagardner.com/cvqual

27 Richard Gardner, *True and False Accusations of Child Sex Abuse,* Creative Therapeutics, 1992, pp 24-25.

28 For example, see Ibid., pp 1-43, 585.

pedophilia, sexual sadism, necrophilia [sex with corpses], zoophilia [sex with animals], coprophilia [sex involving defecation], klismaphilia [sex involving enemas], and urophilia [sex involving urination]. According to him, these things can be seen as having species survival value and "do not warrant being excluded from the list of what are socially acceptable forms of sexual behavior."[29] (Incidentally, Gardner had a genital genetic disorder, hypospadias, that caused a deformation of the penis that required surgical repair of the urethra so that urine is routed through the tip of the penis.)

Gardner professed that "such alternate forms of sexual innovations served nature's purposes by their ability to enhance the general level of sexual excitation in society and thereby increase the likelihood that people will have sex, which then contributes to the survival of the species."[30]

On children being sexual creatures

"There is good reason to believe that most if not all children have the capacity to reach orgasm at the time they are born."[31] He states that some children experience "high sexual urges in early infancy," again a false premise, "and a normal child exhibits a wide variety of sexual fantasies and behaviors, many of which would be labeled as sick or perverted if exhibited in adults."[32]

---

29 Ibid., pp 24-25.
30 *True and False Accusations*, pp 18-32.
31 Ibid., p 15.
32 Richard Gardner, *Sex Abuse Hysteria: Salem Witch Trials Revisited*, Creative Therapeutics, 1991, p 12.

Gardner redefines the relationship between adult and child, incorporating the child as a co-actor and co-conspirator in sexual activity. Gardner denies the victim status of children and promotes a view of children as partners in sexual activities and adults as victims of the children—who are conniving little monsters.[33] This allows the unleashing of a level of hostility toward children that then militates against sympathy for children as victims. Gardner advocates that it is society's puritanical views that create antagonism toward the free expression of sexuality and the importance of early sexualization as a means of promoting the population.[34]

Because Gardner asserts that children experience orgasm, he views damage from the perspective of the failure of gratification from orgasm, the frustration of not reaching climax.[35]

This is an assertion that is medically and scientifically false and with no scientific merit at all. Children do not experience orgasms. The physical necessary biological hormonal development does not take place until puberty. None of this exists in the prepubescent child. These are the fantasies of a psychotic mind, producing a psychotic process. Gardner was an MD, which means he had a scientific understanding of the biological process in humans, but he chose to disregard that knowledge and imagine and promote a functionally psychotic process that does not adhere to science.

---

33 Richard Gardner, Child Custody Litigation: A Guide for Parents and Mental Health Professionals, Creative Therapeutics, 1986. p 93. *True and False Accusations*, pp 12-13

34 *True and False Accusations,* pp 1-43, 525, 670-71.

35 Ibid., p 15.

CHAPTER 10

"The sexually abused child is generally considered to be the victim, but the child may initiate sexual encounters by seducing the adult."[36] When they accomplish the task of seducing an adult into sexual activity and they're caught in the act, then they will accuse the adult of being the perpetrator of engagement, states Gardner.[37] The words written by Gardner, published by his own publishing company, must be viewed as the projections and wishful ravings of a depraved mind written to an audience who seeks support and justification for unconscionable perverted acts of violence and infliction of pain on vulnerable subjects.

On the prevalence and normality of sexual activity in other parts of the world vs. the Western world

Gardner does state that genuine sexual abuse of children is widespread and that over 95% of all sexual abuse allegations are valid.[38] But he also considers sexual activities between adults and children to be a universal phenomenon, which exists to a significant degree around the world in every culture.[39] "Incest is widespread and is probably an ancient tradition."[40] He suggests that the prevalence of this phenomenon is related to the survival of mankind. But a phenomenon existing in large numbers does not mean that it is a good thing.

---

36 Ibid., p 93.
37 *Child Custody Litigation*, p 93.
38 *Sex Abuse Hysteria*, p 149.
39 *True and False Accusations*, p 670.
40 *Sex Abuse Hysteria*, p 119.

Gardner states that Western society is excessively moralistic and punitive toward "atypical" sexual behavior. He states, "The draconian punishments meted out to pedophiles go far beyond what I consider to be the gravity of the crime." He traced the current prohibition of sex between adults and children back to the ancient Jews. He states that it is of interest that of all ancient peoples, it may well be the Jews who were punitive toward pedophiles. "Early Christian proscriptions against pedophilia appear to have been derived from the earlier teachings of the Jews, and our present overreaction to pedophilia represents an exaggeration of Judeo-Christian principles and is a significant factor operative in Western society's atypicality with regard to such activities."[41]

"I too have come to believe that sexual activity between an adult and a child is a reprehensible act. However, I do not believe it is intrinsically so. In other times and societies, it may not be so. The determinate as to whether the experience will be traumatic is a social attitude toward these encounters."[42]

Throughout his treatment recommendations, Gardner repeats that it is the attitude of the public toward adult-child sexual activity that is the determinant of the child's reaction. The view of pedophilia as sickness and crime is simply a reflection of Western societies' position on the subject, he says. "The determinate as to whether the experience will be traumatic is the social attitude toward these encounters."[43]

---

41 *True and False Accusations*, pp 46-47.
42 Ibid., pp 670-671.
43 Ibid., pp 49, 670.

PTSD as desensitization

Gardner states his views on post-traumatic stress disorder (PTSD) as "nature's form of systematic desensitization." "The post-traumatic stress disorder desensitization process involves representation of the trauma verbally, emotionally, and during fantasy play."[44]

The child may become preoccupied with thoughts and feelings about the trauma, but "each time the child relives the experience it becomes a little more bearable." It may help the child to bury the whole incident.[45] Over time the preoccupations diminish and they may become forgotten.[46]

This is again an entirely false premise. PTSD is more like being continually electrocuted, a situation in which the electric shock can reignite at any moment, by whatever glancing memory may retrigger it.

Therapy in cases of child sexual abuse

Gardner does not recommend therapy for sexual abuse cases unless he's 100% convinced the abuse has indeed taken place.[47] He states it is extremely important for a therapist to understand that the child who has been sexually abused may not need intervention. "There is a series of assessments that should be evaluated, and it depends on whether the child was coerced and gained no pleasure and might be considered to

---

[44] Ibid., pp 532, 535.
[45] Richard Gardner, *The Parental Alienation Syndrome*, Creative Therapeutics, 1998, p 75.
[46] *True and False Accusations*, p 536.
[47] *Sex Abuse Hysteria*, p 666.

be raped, to those who enjoyed immensely with orgasmic responses the sexual activities."[48]

He advocates that when a child does go into therapy, a single therapist should be used, and the whole family, including the perpetrator, should be included in the so-called therapy. The therapist who is chosen should have an open mind regarding sexual activity between an adult and a child so that the child does not experience severe psychiatric effects that the therapist may induce in the treatment environment.[49]

He blames therapists for introducing the bias that any sexual encounter between an adult and a child "however short, no matter how tender, loving, and non-painful, automatically and predictably must be psychologically traumatic to the child."[50]

This is all counterintuitive and illogical. These traumatic experiences unfold over some time with developing consciousness and awareness of the implications of the nature of the sexual exchange between an adult and a child. The reverberations take place through all stages of the life process as the child develops into an adult, shaping and intruding upon the free and unimpaired development of interpersonal relationships involving trust, personal judgment, and decision-making.

Therapy should be spent talking about other things, he says, as the goal is to help people forget about their problems.[51] The goal of therapy should be to facilitate the

---

48 *True and False Accusations*, pp 535, 548.
49 Ibid., p 528.
50 Ibid., 670-671.
51 Ibid., p 592.

desensitization process, not artificially prolong it with "psychotherapeutic muckraking." He advocates that if the child feels guilty about participating, the child is told that in other societies such behavior is normal and our society has an exaggerated punitive response. "Older children may be helped to appreciate that sexual encounters between adult and child are not universally considered to be reprehensible acts. The child might be told about other societies in which such behavior was and is considered normal. The child might be helped to appreciate the wisdom of Shakespeare's *Hamlet*, 'Nothing's either good or bad, but thinking makes it so.'"[52]

Gardner believes that fathers who deny committing sexual molestation should be engaged in therapy. If the father desires treatment, the therapist should focus on enhancing his self-esteem. This is accomplished by helping him understand that "there is a bit of pedophilia in every one of us" (1991, p 118) and "pedophilia has been considered to be the norm by the vast majority of individuals in the history of the world." In our society, because we take a punitive attitude toward these inclinations, "he has had a certain amount of bad luck with regard to the place and time he had been born."[53]

In addition to feeling sorry for his misfortune, the father should be helped to feel pity for the child for being born "in a society that considers his behavior a heinous crime and/or a mortal sin."[54]

Gardner advocates that fathers have to be helped to see that although pedophilia is accepted in other cultures, this

---

52 Ibid., 549.
53 Ibid., p 593.
54 Ibid., p 592.

does not justify this practice in our society, even though our society overacts to it. "It is because our society overreacts to it that children suffer," he reminds us yet again.[55]

"The removal of a pedophilic parent from the home should be seriously considered after all attempts to first be given the opportunity for community treatment. If that then fails, only then should some sort of forced incarceration be considered."[56] He states that although the child could be protected from further abuse, the therapist should not alienate the child from the molesting parent.[57]

And what of the protective parent in therapy? Assuming it is the mother, Gardner says, "If the mother has reacted to the abuse in a hysterical fashion, or used it as an excuse for a campaign of denigration of the father, then the therapist does well to try and 'sober her up.' ... Her hysterics ... will contribute to the child's feeling that a heinous crime has been committed and will thereby lessen the likelihood of any kind of rapprochement with the father. One has to do everything possible to help her put the 'crime' in proper perspective. She has to be helped to appreciate that in most societies in the history of the world, such behavior was ubiquitous and this is still the case."[58]

Gardner says that in therapy perhaps the mother "can be helped to understand that in the history of the world his behavior has been more common than the restrained behavior of those who do not sexually abuse their children."[59]

---

55 Ibid, p 594-5.
56 *Sex Abuse Hysteria*, p 119.
57 *True and False Accusations*, p 537.
58 Ibid., pp 576-7.
59 Ibid., p 588.

More on how the protective parents should respond

Gardner blames the mother and the child for the father's sexual abuse. "It may be that one of the reasons the daughter turned toward the father is the impairment of the child's relationship with the mother."[60]

His writing says that the protective parent should be discouraged from involving herself with litigation, as it will interfere with the child's natural "desensitization" process, and it will subject the child to interrogations that will inevitably be damaging.[61] Moreover, legal investigations of the trauma may cause more damage to the child than what was done by the abuse.[62]

Maybe the mother can protect her daughter by increasing her own sexuality, according to Gardner. "Her own diminished guilt over masturbation will make it easier for her to encourage the practice in her daughter, if this is warranted. And her increased sexuality may lessen the need for her husband to return to their daughter for sexual gratification."[63]

The fact that feelings may be shared between the child and the preferred parent, for Gardner, de-legitimizes the credibility of the child. The empathic parent is not, then, an individual who understands what the child is feeling, or simply experiences a shared reality. For Gardner, any breach in forcing the child to a compliant position of adherence to the authority of the rejected parent, is an act of supporting alienation.[64]

---

60 Ibid., p 579-80.
61 Ibid., p 577.
62 *The Parental Alienation Syndrome*, p 75.
63 *True and False Accusations*, p 585.
64 Ibid.

Conclusion

The Gardner concepts of "parental alienation" were generated by personal pathology, prejudice, and marketing sales pitches to defend the indefensible acts of child sexual abusers, and predators who sought out Gardner's services as a forensic expert. Gardner's core group of 300 clients involved men who had been accused of incest and sexual abuse of children.

When Gardner states that sexual abuse claims cause more damage to the child than the act itself, Gardner projects onto others tactics that he employs: coercion, manipulation of facts, and leading questions, as he deploys counterintuitive theories, counter to the direct experience of children exposed to adult sexual activity, and counter to scientific and medical knowledge and evidence.

This cruel aberration of a therapeutic process is based on the fantasies of a psychotic, deranged individual who has ascended as a force in the legal field because of its usefulness in defending criminals for profit. The "parental alienation" movement in the family courts is driven by an amoral legal system that has embraced the benefits of reasonable doubt to exonerate child abuse criminals and transfer children into the hands of abusers.

Gardner suggests that the promotion of sexual abuse allegations is the product of "national hysteria" motivated by a drive for power and money, a clear projection and transference of Gardner's motives and actual accomplishment of creating a cottage industry around parental alienation: the defense of some 400 clients accused of incest.[65]

---

[65] Richard Gardner, "Clinical Evaluation of Alleged Child Sex Abuse in Custody Disputes," *Innovations in Clinical Practice: A Source Book*, Volume 7, edited by Peter A. Keller and Steven R. Heyman, 1988, pp 61-76.

The motive of profit, driven by child support from federal funds into state coffers, underwrites the perversions of a racist pedophile-promotor who essentially said that children are born as sexual creatures and child sexual abuse doesn't exist. These false concepts are antithetical to a society that respects the rights and privileges of individuals to protect children. But these concepts, which are counter to science, biology, and respect for human autonomy and self-direction, are used as the basis of the aberrant and deviant incursions of those who wish to assert arrogant false premises in the family court system.

The imposition of aberrant psychopathic behaviors should under no circumstances be canonized and driven into the public arena by a drive for autocratic control and personal financial gain, but this is where we are: the current American court system is driven by the psychotic ravings of a psychopathic, racist pedophile-protector.

All of Richard Gardner's concepts of adult-child sexual activity, as well as his concept of "parental alienation" can be represented by one Nathan Larson, an accountant from Charlottesville, Virginia, who ran for Congress in 2018. Larson publicly describes himself as a pedophile who raped his ex-wife repeatedly during their marriage, before her suicide. Larson describes his longing to have sex with his three-year-old daughter but is constrained from doing so because he "relinquished [his] parental rights during a custody battle."[66] Mr. Larson is a somewhat extreme member of the continuum of examples of the

---

[66] Jesselyn Cook and Andy Campbell, "Congressional Candidate in Virginia Admits He's a Pedophile," *HuffPost*, May 31, 2018. https://www.huffpost.com/entry/nathan-larson-congressional-candidate-pedophile_n_5b10916de4b0d5e89e1e4824.

predator population, represented in the real-time, real-life videotapes of adult men detached from the agony of screaming babies as their adult genitals are pushed into baby parts.

Each time court actors deny that child abuse is being committed, because of wrangling over verbiage created to cover acts of depravity instead of looking at the clinical behavior and statements of children, they risk condemning the subjects to extraordinary damage. Psychobabble that pretends to accurately portray a family dynamic should not be allowed to take the place of real behavior and the real communications of children.

The destruction of generations of children is an atrocity driven by hypocrisy and fear of criticism for what appear to be unpopular views. It is allowed by the failure of well-known and well-respected professionals to shout from the battlements that this theory, this philosophy undermines a safe and civilized society.

Though other professionals are not speaking up about this, the destructive nature of these concepts is strongly criticized by the experts of the Foundation for Child Victims of the Family Courts.

Chapter 11

Similarities Between Richard Gardner and NAMBLA

NAMBLA, the North American Man/Boy Love Association, is a pedophilia and pederasty advocacy organization founded in 1978. The similarities between the theories touted by Gardner and those promoted by NAMBLA are worth noting.

While Gardner railed against mandated reporting, NAMBLA's mission "Men Loving Boys Loving Men" is to eradicate age of consent laws that criminalize adult sexual involvement with minors. NAMBLA has campaigned for the release of men who have been imprisoned for sexual contact with minors that they viewed as not involving coercion.

The arguments NAMBLA uses about mutual sexual relationships between men and boys,[67] such as asserting that prepubescent children have a sexual drive and feel sexual arousal and excitement and are gratified by the sexual act, find their roots in the same false premises examined in the previous chapter related to the origins of childhood sexuality that do not exist. They do not exist

---

67 NAMBLA.org.

because the biological processes of sexual arousal and drive, the hormones and receptors, have not been developed. The light has not hit the pineal gland, and the organisms that are generated by the process that becomes ignited are not in existence. One may make arguments that the earth is flat, but the epistemological evidence to support such conjecture is not there.

Like Gardner, NAMBLA refers to critics of sexual activity between adults and children as hypocritical, denying natural human instincts and repressing children's natural drives,[68] those same "natural drives" falsely asserted for the self-serving, manipulative motives of the predators who insist on redefining nature and anatomy for their selfish purposes.

NAMBLA proposes that non-violent sexual activity between adults and children is a positive experience, that there is no harm or injury, and that children are not traumatized by the adult imposition of sexual acts. The harm, they say, comes from the attitudes of the uninformed that instill guilt and fear in children.[69] As the previous chapter showed, Gardner utilizes the same false narratives.

Appeal to higher loyalties is described by both NAMBLA and Gardner in terms of an appeal to the liberation of children from repressive sexual mores in the name of freedom of expression in behavior and speech.[70] The promotion of these concepts has tried to sidestep

---

68 Mary deYoung, "The World According to NAMBLA: Accounting for Deviance," The Journal of Sociology * Social Welfare, 1989, 16(1), Article 9.
69 deYoung, "The indignant page: Techniques of neutralization in the publications of pedophile organizations," *Child Abuse & Neglect,* 12(4), 1988, 583-91.
70 *True and False Accusations*, pp 1-43, 585.

the true self-serving, manipulative nature of individuals and groups that have sought to justify the willingness to negate the pain and suffering of others to engage in their pleasure as well as justifying and even glorifying their false premises.

Gardner's premises, so parallel to those of NAMBLA, generated the psychotically-based theory of "parental alienation syndrome." The legal profession then embraced this theory and ran with it, despite the clear evidence that the premises on which it is based are disembodied from facts and science. For them, it provided the "reasonable doubt" they needed, even though it was based on an unreasonable theory—a theory that was even disconnected from reason—regarding the dynamics that exist between vulnerable children and adults.

The work of Richard Gardner, MD, served to provide an identity and a way forward for cases that would have languished in contentious, difficult litigation or would have been referred for criminal prosecution.

Chapter 12

Weaponizing Gardner's "Parental Alienation Syndrome" Theory in the Courts

The "tender years doctrine" of the past taught that in cases of child custody, young children should automatically go to their mothers, which sometimes meant that good fathers would be locked out of their children's lives altogether. As time passed, studies increasingly showed the importance of children having healthy male parents in their lives.

The Father's Rights movement, born in the early 1990s as a reaction to the tender years' doctrine, countered it with reasonable arguments for shared parenting. Fathers' rights advocates reasonably asserted that family courts were biased toward women. They argued that even if the fathers were better parents, these courts gave mothers automatic custody and child support.

The new plan was to develop a one-size-fits-all "shared parenting" plan. Eventually, family courts adopted what they called a "fair standard" of decision-making, even a "best interest of the child" standard. This new standard was ostensibly objective, guided by a psychological evaluation of both parents. Psychological evaluations, with their supposed character diagnoses and "family pathology scale," provided the illusion of objectivity.

But the truth is that these evaluations are highly subjective. Notoriously the system of evaluation has been without the oversight of any validity, credibility, reliability, accuracy, or truth standard guided by professionals.

The pendulum that was trying to swing to a balance continued to swing, all the way to another extreme, along the lines of Gardner's "parental alienation" theory. And so, in family courts, mothers who made accusations of child abuse against the fathers were labeled as monsters, while the accused were labeled the victims.

Over years of growing power, the political, legal, and social organizations trumpeting "fathers' rights" have managed to produce family courts that have become units of organized crime. A movement that was intended to protect fathers' rights to be with their children has become a financially powerful system in which "fathers' rights" include the right to abuse their children.

Gardner's writing about child sexual abuse and his parental alienation concept has been critiqued by many within the legal and psychological profession (e.g., Joan Meier Esq. PA & PAS, A Research Review, Sept. 2013). Even those theorists and practitioners who embrace the Gardner concept of alienation (e.g., Richard Warshak, Ph.D., *Divorce Poison*, 2001) agree to the caveat that where real abuse has taken place, a child has every right to reject the abuser. But the argument remains that the alleged abuse did not take place.

Over the years Gardner successfully presided over some 400 custody evaluations, transferring children into the hands of their alleged abusers.[71] Even his 2003 suicide did not dampen the appetite of court actors across the land from developing the concept of "parental alienation" into a psychological and legal windfall. Now there was a tool to separate "good" parents from "bad" parents. And how are these "bad parents" identified? Not as child abusers. But as "alienators."

Gardner and those who subscribe to his junk concept of parental alienation suggest that a child's antipathy to a rejected parent stems from the "programming," manipulation, and "brainwashing" of a child by the parent designated as preferred by the child—the parent accusing of abuse.[72]

Gardner's theory of parental alienation created a simple good/bad standard by which custody decisions can be judged and rapidly implemented, so cases can continue to be moved through the family court system, full speed ahead, without thought of the destruction being left in the wake.

The problem of child sexual abuse—the most widespread, under-reported crime in our society, and among the most troublesome matters in dealing with custody decisions—was simply redefined in terms of "perception."

The explosive popularity of the Gardner theories of how sexual abuse is not sexual abuse but a cultural phenomenon of prejudice has created an environment of equal opportunity for both men and women to exploit sexual abuse. Terms used to medically and scientifically define and operationalize concepts that demonstrate or

---

71 Richard Gardner, CV, http://richardagardner.com/cvqual.
72 *Child Custody Litigation*, p 2.

explain what constitutes sexual abuse and why these acts are harmful, physically and emotionally, with consequences that evolve and reverberate throughout the life cycle, have been manipulated by the Gardner propagandists to project many normal sexual and interpersonal developmental behaviors displayed by children. Gardner has manipulated and associated normal, developmental behaviors of children engaged in through play, interpersonal testing, for socialization, communication, and learning through play and imitation, and has redefined those normal acts as perversions or conscious acts of seduction and entrapment of adults for malevolent purposes.

The mass consumption and normalization of theories that are immoral, unreasonable, unscientific, and counterintuitive have reached an epidemic level. A mask of sanity generated by seemingly educated licensed professionals has overtaken the public consciousness, disseminating madness as the norm. Those we should most fear and remove from power are immunizing public literacy against the standard of that which is genocide.

PART FOUR

Behind the Iron Curtain in the Family Courts

Chapter 13

High-Conflict Custody Situations in Family Court

Internal categories of client custody challenges

Statistics indicate that a very high percentage of divorce cases are settled reasonably, amicably, and without the lurid, despicable facts that accompany the cases dealt with by the FCVFC. The FCVFC is concerned exclusively with those high-conflict case situations in which there are multiple issues of inequity within the immediate family unit that raise concerns about children being transferred by the family courts across the United States from the protective parent into the hands of a documented parent abuser.

Court proceedings, within each court as well as across the United States in separate jurisdictions, are not consistent or subject to uniform oversight or review. Regarding judicial discretion and the authority of judicial immunity, qualified and absolute immunity are unique factors that impact the power balance of judicial decision-making and therefore create unique challenges to argument and evidence preparation, particularly where there is a compelling interest to protect subject children against abuse.

Sometimes parents self-sabotage who indeed need to seek custody of vulnerable children facing the transfer of custody into the isolation of a well-documented abuser. But in this section, I will address issues that deal with the litigants' relationship with the court in the process of seeking equitable distribution of marital assets and protection of children.

In some cases, spouses have engaged in bad acts and have made bad decisions, and some have faced very serious consequences in their lives, relationships, and marriages. But in many of these cases, these parents still love their children, want the best for them, and are not a danger to them. Their children clearly show love for these parents and want to be with them.

When there is true remorse on the part of the offending person, not engaging in "yes but" behavior, when there is a true desire to work on the issues raised in the intimate secrets beyond the divorce complaint, then the parent is a safe parent for the children and may be seen and trusted as a candidate in good faith for intensive personal psychotherapy and family therapy

These parents should share parenting time with their children with parameters and thresholds for advancement as supported by all family participants in such treatment decisions. However, there are parents whose motives for seeking custody of children involve covering secrets related to predatory behavior, revenge for the rejection of the parent seeking protection of themselves or their children, or motives related to financial enrichment and acquisition of marital assets.

The experts associated with the FCVFC have seen a clear pattern of institutional avarice, greed, and a Darwinian level of survival of the fittest court agency growth as it comes to drawing federal funding through state agency incentives for child support. State and governmental agencies paired with the financial incentives of professionally hired guns to increase their salaries via providing services to a captive audience of litigants create a perfect storm for mass corruption. In the experience of the FCVFC experts, the operative years of the Gardner insemination of false narratives beginning in the 1980s through the present, along with the intensive ramping up of abject fear in a captive court audience, creates a perfect storm for more control of vulnerable subjects and ongoing generational destruction assisted by the dumbing down of the public consciousness.

When one spouse is an abuser...

The situation changes, or should change, when one parent has engaged in criminal behavior, such as domestic violence, child sexual abuse, or any other form of child endangerment. Questions as to proof of culpability are critical; however, the court's willingness to accept and respond to proofs of dangerousness and the feelings and complaints of the child has proven to be problematic in courts that take a paranoid stance, viewing each complaint by a parent as a lie and seeking an advantage that then seems to automatically roll over to the benefit of the parent accused of crimes against a child. The position of automatic joint custody and equal decision-making are preferred positions.

In cases of both domestic violence and child abuse, the non-offending parent who loves the abuser but is confused about the abuser's behavior, unfamiliar with concepts such as gaslighting and coercive control, can unwittingly harm their case by not presenting the problems that have caused the initiation of the divorce. When the parent has been in denial or living in wishful thinking and is forced to present a strong case, a sudden change in positions may be viewed with suspicion.

In some cases, the children and protective parents have been raped, beaten, humiliated, and deprived of education or medical care. In far too many cases, the abuser is even a psychopathic predator who can instill terror in the hearts of well-socialized victims. These psychopaths threaten the opposition with being unable to prove the heinous, despicable acts that they are committing against the victims they hold in their possession.

We also see predatory pedophiles who choose naïve spouses to bear children for them that they can then use for their perverted carnal ends.

Psychopathic predators, not unlike serial killers, love to hide in plain sight, to demonstrate how clever they are and how stupid everyone else is. They often portray themselves as a victim, elaborating on their stories of anguish, of being maligned, abused, and financially used. They take pleasure in seeing how easily they can manipulate others to gain support and sympathy for their plight.

These predator hypocrites congratulate themselves on words received from law enforcement. "You should sue her for all that she says about you." This makes them feel invincible, elated with power, and grandiose in their threats. They laugh at the police, who sympathize with them instead of serving and protecting helpless children, children whom they have been called to rescue, or spouses who have been threatened and beaten but bruises are not yet visible.

The protective parent, who may begin to understand the dilemma, also experiences confusion, fear, grief, anger, and self-doubt.

Most often, the worst of child abuse happens in secret. Before the child develops the skills of managing a complex living environment and challenges way beyond his capacities, he is forced to develop coping mechanisms to deal with his survival. The child's psyche must mediate the view of the abuser, in order to encompass the emotions of intense fear, hatred, helplessness, and the need to come to terms with coping with his oppressor who now has control of his being.

In one of many such instances, sisters could not escape the screams of their toddler half-sister taken into a room by their father. Behind closed doors, there would be about 5 seconds of a blood-curdling scream. It would stop, and there would be no sound. They thought she might be dead and then the blood-curdling scream began again, several times. Eventually, their father would come from the room, leaving the child alone. The child would be silent, leaving her sisters to fear that she was dead. They could do nothing because the court officials did not believe them and would not even investigate. The FCVFC became involved and helped procure the freedom of one sister still in the father's custody.

If your child reports sexual abuse at the hands of the other parent

There are many ways in which children disclose sexual abuse, and it is rarely in a direct, articulate manner though the communication is generally quite clear to the listener. The response of the listener to the child is critical in soliciting information, taking corrective action, and making sure to understand the meaning of the words the child is using to describe an event or interaction, as well as the accompanying affect associated with the child's disclosure.

A two-year-old girl said to her mother, quite cheerfully, "Daddy put his wee wee in my pee pee." The interpretation of those words commenced a devastating criminal investigation that ended with a clarification of the event described. The child was trying to communicate her amusement that her father urinated in the toilet that she left unflushed after she had urinated (peed). Interpretation—Daddy put his wee wee (urinated in the toilet) in my pee pee (my urine that was in the toilet). The importance of children being taught proper names of body parts and body functions is clear from this example, in addition to the need for rather detailed explanations of the child's thoughts and experiences. Further, it must be built into all forensic evaluations that time, patience, and careful support for eliciting the meaning of a child's words are central to all child forensic interviews, which should be audio and video taped to allow for critical review.

Chapter 3 told the story of Crystal, the twenty-two-month-old girl who was subject to her father coming into her bedroom at night, removing her diaper, pulling down his underwear (white cotton briefs), pulling off her diaper, and rubbing his penis against her vagina. When the child began screaming every time the father came near her, the child's mother became alarmed. The child was extremely intelligent and articulate and demonstrated a reasoning capacity way beyond her years. When she stated in session, "Why did he do that to me?" it only remained to ask questions. Her affect was one of extreme distress, accompanied by body rocking as well as crawling, moving forward and then backing up, moving forward and backing up.

Let's lay out the scenario of a child disclosing/indicating to one parent that the child was exposed to or actively engaged in sexual interaction with the other parent. Inadvertent comments may suggest that the child has been exposed to inappropriate touching, and looking, along with being told, "do not tell." The child may indicate that they have been told that something that hurts or is frightening to them is a good thing, normal, or part of the parent's responsibility to expose the child to, in order to teach them.

Sometimes a child will react to something they see with surprisingly intense emotion. One three-year-old girl screamed and cried when a midwife came to the family home and was preparing a routine external examination of the child's very pregnant mother. The child yelled and screamed for the midwife not to touch her mother so that her mother would not be harmed.

Upon discussion and reassurance of the child that there was no harm, this outburst provided the dawning awareness on the part of the mother that her once happy precocious little one was being exposed to something of which the mother was not aware but needed to become enlightened. From this moment of concern commenced an inquiry that would produce a horrifying tale of child sexual abuse via intergenerational cult activity amid an upper-middle-class community where the father was an accountant and member of an exclusive business firm. The extended family involved in horrendous allegations of cult sexual activity were church members with church leaders who were famous for their missionary work in the Caribbean Islands, along with engagement in developing and supporting orphanages.

When one is alerted to any form of concern about the prospect of abuse, sexual or otherwise, one must first think about changes in the child's overall functioning—eating, sleeping, bowel functions, and mood. One must look for patterns of regression—developmental stages mastered and then lost. If there is not a significant biological explanation for a child who has been toilet trained and then progressively loses bowel functioning, or any other developmental marker grasped and then abandoned, along with other significant personality changes—displays of anger, depression, withdrawal—one needs to look more deeply into what is going on in this child's life within the family, daycare, school, and let no one dissuade you from your research.

Normalizing that which is abnormal, suggesting that "this behavior is a phase" is an indulgence in the convenient rationalization that your child cannot afford. Symptoms of abuse or grooming behavior need to be recognized even when that grooming behavior is portrayed as fun. ("We love taking baths with Daddy and washing him all over and having him wash us all over.") Grooming and preparing a child for the next steps for further inculcation into physical sexual engagement may not appear as traumatic, but it is a road to "normalizing" a child into a dysfunctional, aberrant manner of functioning while keeping the child in complete ignorance about what they are doing.

One father came to his four-year-old's bed at night, massaging her and stroking her vagina. He told her to go up to her teacher and grab her breasts because her teacher would think that that was funny and they would have a good laugh. The outcome of that escapade did not go well, and the child was devastated and confused when she got into trouble. The consequences of behaviors and advice that conflict, cause confusion, and are counterintuitive to the child are consistent with the abuser's malevolent intentions toward the child, namely, the intention to make the child not credible and to make the child not trust their judgments or feelings as well as undermining the child's overall trust in everyone.

Among the most egregious acts of judicial damage is the undermining of the authority of protective parents and the right of children to in fact be protected against harm. A court system's implementation of a disembodied, unscientific, improbable abstract theory that restricts the reporting of crimes undermines all credibility and authority of the court system to be assigned authority and any right to rule in the public interest.

An autocratic rule that seeks nothing more than its own financial increase and authoritarian control is a danger to the entire social structure. The ability of the family to protect children, and to protect their financial integrity is entirely undermined by the assembly line functioning of court proceedings implementing Gardner's theories related to the denial of sexual abuse of children and the criminalization of parents who seek to protect themselves and their children.

Incest is a crime, yet often a disclosure is hushed up because of social and financial upheaval caused to family stability. The shame of the crime taints all associated. It is understandable for the non-offending parent to want to avoid dealing with such an accusation. However, because of the potential for incalculable harm to the child, any sort of sexual interaction must be taken very seriously. As soon as there are warning signs, notifications, and disclosures of child sexual abuse in any form, the protective parent must take proper action.

If you are the protective parent, you may think that a child's disclosure of sexual abuse would make child custody for you an open and shut case. But it most certainly is not. At the same time, nondisclosure of any form of abuse or endangerment is of equal and or greater harm. The source of the problem has to do with the integrity of the court and operatives involved in the legal process, which is why the court in every aspect, every manifestation of its functioning must be held accountable by addressing and redressing procedural, due process, and constitutional violations that harm the righteous deliberation of cases before every deliberation.

Looking for help in family court

If a complaint of child sexual abuse were to be lodged against a non-family member, the motive might be questioned, but the complaint would not be immediately dismissed. The complaint would most likely be reviewed and even investigated.

However, in family court, the circumstances are very different. In family court, maintaining the illusion of family support takes precedence over child welfare. "Having a relationship" with an abuser is seen as far more important than the mental health of traumatized children.

Thus, the well-known response to allegations of sexual abuse involving parenting partners is for authorities to discount the complaint of the complainant, to dispute, challenge, and deny them. Far more work goes into challenging and disproving the allegations than into listening to the victims and investigating their evidence.

The fact of the matter is that as child sexual abuse increases in the United States (including grooming and coercive control of victims under the authority of an abuser), so are the perverse rulings of the courts, transferring children into the hands of abusers.

The problem of "no-fault" divorce

No-fault divorce was originally posed as a way to facilitate independent decision-making, allowing couples to dissolve a contract that was no longer beneficial to them. The two litigants are treated as equals, both blameless partners who have simply changed their minds about the desire to be married and wish to alter the marriage contract.

This may be true for a significant portion of the population. However, in cases in which "fault" is an issue—cases in which abuse precipitated the need for a divorce and protection of children—those cases have formed an arena in which criminals are protected and should be prosecuted through the legal system.

Now, family court judges, who are untrained in criminal matters, are put in the position of having to decide matters involving crimes. These judges and other court actors are not equipped to deal with matters of evidence production and submission or understand how and why the behavior in a given situation constitutes a crime.

What constitutes pornography? What constitutes grooming behavior as associated with child sexual abuse? Issues of interpersonal violence, and coercive control, all of these are terms understood in the criminal court system but are inappropriate for the family court system.

No-fault divorce has become a vehicle for allowing the acting out of behavior that would normally be defined as criminal acts.

As the situation now stands, the criminal division of the court system has ceded much of its authority to family courts, thus eviscerating and undermining their authority to prosecute criminals. Crime victims who have the ill fate of being subjected to the family courts instead of the criminal courts are unable to seek protection from crimes committed against them because judges in family courts exonerate the criminal.

The bias of family court judges and their appointed factotum

Clinical investigation and extensive research consistently indicate that crimes of a violent and obscene nature are more likely to take place between family members because of access and an environment that assumes a basic level of intimacy and trust.

However, despite this well-known fact, family court litigants with a significant charge of criminal behavior are immediately met with suspicion. This is because a closely held opinion in custody litigation is that subjects in divorce and custody litigation will falsify and exaggerate claims to secure an advantage with the court.

But not only are they met with suspicion. Those litigants who come to court with serious, legitimate complaints, with evidence, have in the past 25 years fared far worse than those who simply keep their mouths shut.

In family court, where criminals seek shelter through the manipulation of a court process that should be examining alleged dangerous behavior, the entire court process has been designed to dismiss even the idea that criminal behavior ever existed. These foregone conclusions lead to the presumption that raising issues of serious criminal behavior is done to discredit the other party, seeking to distort and manipulate the entire proceeding.

The family court has become an arena governed more by judicial discretion than actual law. But rather than "discretion," what we are seeing is indiscretion, abuse of power, abuse of process, and virtually no oversight, thus creating an environment of profiteering tantamount to the practice of child trafficking.

Chapter 14

Jaw-Dropping Antics in Family Court

Very few, if any, protective parents facing custody litigation defending against abuse (which should be addressed in criminal court) have any idea what they are facing. They hope that through cooperation with the process, the court will come to understand the truth of the situation being litigated, and justice will be done.

How wrong they are.

Weaponizing the "parental alienation" theory

Parental alienation has been and continues to be rejected by the premiere authority on mental health evaluation, the Diagnostic and Statistical Manual of Mental Disorders, 5th Edition (DSM 5). Parental alienation is not even considered in the section on disorders needing further research.

Despite this fact, courts across the country have embraced the "parental alienation" protocol and are increasingly following the directives of false profits. Marketing campaigns on behalf of parental alienation practitioners publicize and market their custody "wins" to audiences of attorneys. They stress that attorneys need to engage parental alienation practitioners in order to learn litigation techniques that support the arguments of parental alienation.

Judges and entire court systems are embracing a perverted, destructive cult organized to usurp and reorganize judicial authority from fact to fiction, from court to non-judicial authorities, empowering them to make fundamental evidentiary determinations.

Most court actors have no idea of the dark genesis of Richard Gardner's "parental alienation" theories. But they do know that "parental alienation" expedites the litigation process in high-conflict cases.

Accordingly, since the early 2000s, the FCVFC has seen a growing pattern of the development of a cottage industry of "parental alienation assessment experts." They give wings to the litigation strategy of "parental alienation" associated with shaming and blaming victims and protective parents.

The courts then use this strategy to add layers of legal maneuverings to the case, making complicated that which should have been straightforward, clear, and indisputable.

Which one is the criminal?

In matters of accusations of child abuse, two questions are paramount:

1. Is the matter under consideration a crime?
2. If so, is the accused responsible for the crime?

In criminal court, the judge and jury would ideally weigh evidence, listen to testimony, and draw a reasonable conclusion.

If this were a criminal court, with court professionals who are true to their professional skills, professional competence, and fiduciary responsibility, we would find that the majority of these cases can yield clear and convincing evidence. But this is not a criminal court. This is family court. So instead, they present an alternate "reality" created through the presence of a mass of conflicting, confusing information generated by the person accused of heinous crimes.

The family court cut-and-paste edited version of the Gardner doctrine says that there can only be two types of parents: jealous, toxic accuser parent, or innocent accused parent. Abuse accusations are simply and always false statements geared to gain an advantage by one parent over another.

This version has been propelled by the profitable industry of fraudulent psychological and psychiatric evaluators who develop reports that lie, distort, misrepresent, offer false histories, and create findings of toxic diagnoses against the targeted parent and a cleaned-up version of twisted history that advances a false narrative.

This cover-up of crimes has generated a massive industry vested in stating that all mentions of inter-family crimes against children are false. Children coming forward to report crimes are liars, coached by a parent who is seeking an unauthorized advantage in whatever proceedings are moving forward.

Statistics indicate that far more people have experienced sexual assault than come forward in reporting. But family court actors ignore the science that studies and describes child sexual abuse. In fact, they have wrapped their arms around the "reasonable doubt" element raised by Gardner's theory that sexual abuse does not exist and that the parent raising this claim is doing so out of spite and malice.

"Parental alienation" accommodates the litigation skill of arguing both sides of an argument with the goal of total obfuscation of the central issue—assigning guilt to the correct party. In this way, high-conflict custody litigation can be written off as a "he said/she said," non-fact-based circular argument.

Buzzwords that have no intellectual content, scientific basis, or documented evidence are floated to support the illegitimate, baseless theory advanced by greed-driven, unethical practitioners. The terms "alienation" and "coaching" have taken on a life of their own now as the condensed terms in and of themselves may be held up as flash cards to warn litigants never to raise allegations of sexual abuse, or for that matter allegations of any other forms of abuse, except of course "parental alienation," that most heinous abuse of all.

"Parental alienation" gives a prescription for the protective parent to be demonized to cover for a parent who has subjected a child to harm. The overwhelming theme of this form of intervention is the suppression of claims, evidence, and witnesses of heinous crimes against children.

In the majority of cases, the protective parent, the one who has alleged abuse and seeks to defend, will lose their children to the predator parent. Thus, if you say, "my child was abused," custody will most likely transfer to the accused abuser. No defense or presentation of evidence is necessary. The accuser is mocked as a liar, as are the children. The accused abuser, on the other hand, is exonerated by the mere mouthing of claims that children are being abused.

The anti-intellectual, anti-morality concept of "parental alienation" has been opening the gates of hell for protective parents to lose their children to abusers as soon as they call attention to child abuse of any kind.

Equal opportunity enablers

The family courts of the 21st century do not lean simply toward fathers who are accused of abuse. No, these courts are equal opportunity enablers and will now order that the children be given to whichever parent is accused of abuse and be taken from whichever parent is making the accusation, the "alienator."

Not only through what they learn in school, but also through whim and malevolent cruelty, family court judges across the country are arranging for protective parents of either sex to lose their children. Instead of truly examining the evidence, instead of truly listening to the children, U.S. family courts are systematically punishing the wrong person and turning children over to their abusers.

When a parent raises charges of abuse in the course of marital litigation, that parent will be judged, and all due process will be shut down by familiar court protocol. This protocol consists of actions of abuse in the court system: coercive controls, threats, and intimidation tactics, which not only are brutally destructive to all innocent parties but also elevate the accused abuser to a place of sympathy and a prejudgment of innocence. The protective parent is no longer a litigant in a court process, but a victim of an obscene playing out of a process that leads to the transfer of vulnerable children into the control of their abuser.

Commonly in the family courts, the judge will make a *sua sponte* order (that is, an order made by the judge without any prompting from anyone else). The judge will order psychological evaluations for both parents and will command that the results of the evaluations be sealed from the targeted parent—the parent who is about to lose custody. This parent will almost invariably be the one who has made the allegation of child abuse.

The targeted parent will then have no idea as to the content of the report about themselves, the other parent, or their children. As a result, they are left shadowboxing, trying to figure out what has been written about them and rushing to try to refute what they have come to realize are false allegations... against themselves.

The child victims are often suspended for years, isolated in the custody of abusers who control the narratives both by intimidating witnesses and/or lining the ranks of professionals—lawyers, clinicians, evaluators, with those who are equally willing to lie, cheat, and steal to bury the truth. Perpetrators of harm hope that victims who endure will fade into the woodwork and move beyond time limits for prosecution—lost to statutes of limitations for reporting even the most heinous of crimes.

Intimidating children with "reunification therapy"

The process in family court in cases of abuse allegations is usually as follows:

1. In custody litigation, a complaint of abuse is lodged and responded to.
2. The "team" is appointed.
3. "Evaluation" takes place.
4. "Treatment" is assigned.
5. Visitation is scheduled.
6. When the children express their dismay, anger, and fear at being left alone with one they have named as an abuser, custody is transferred from the "alienator" (the protective parent) to the "alienated" (the alleged abuser).
7. If the children continue to protest, they may be assigned to a "therapeutic reunification program."

The perceived need to keep the children in a relationship with their abuser gave rise to the "reunification" model of responding to children who—with good cause and compelling evidence—are resisting the parent they wanted to flee.

Under these circumstances, there can be no "reunification," because there was never "unification" in the first place.

But the conviction behind "reunification therapy" is that whatever the charges are against an accused parent, they're not true. These accusations, according to the "reunification" model, simply come from a disgruntled (protective) parent who is jealous and competitive with the right of the other parent to exercise control, physical and psychological, which includes sexual access to the child.

After children have sought refuge from abusers—with statements and documentation of heinous physical and sexual abuse—this "reunification therapy" program uses tactics of coercive control to force children into the exclusive custody of those very abusers.

Family Bridges, one example of a "reunification therapy" provider, has no base of operations and no academic profile in terms of what its theory and philosophy are and who are the personnel who are enacting it, aside from the psychologist Randy Rand, who lost his license to practice psychology.

These "reunification programs" are unlicensed, undefined programs promoted as something like summer camps with family values. What they are in reality is more like a military brainwashing program run by the juvenile justice system, in which the child's thinking is reprogrammed to the will of the litigation team in charge.

The "reunification" process is driven by a court order that empowers the program to authorize "transfer agents"—thugs with court authority—to pick up the children from wherever they are: hospitals, mental institutions, correctional facilities, or custody of the other parent. The "rapid response team" of transporters comes as armed guards to collect and remove children, if need be, by private planes across state lines and across the country.

They are then taken to a hotel room where they will be confronted alone, without an attorney, protective parent, or another advocate. The only other people there besides the child will be the "reunification specialist" team and the accused parent, who has gained access through the court.

With the assistance of the reunification team, this parent can inform the children that the abuse they reported never existed but rather is the product of the villainous scheme of the other parent (who they were "deceived into believing" was their protector) and that this vindictive "protective parent" only wanted to interfere with the relationship of the parent who is now seeking access to and control over them.

Children are told that if they don't cooperate and conform to the program, then the parent who is opposing the program will go to jail for the rest of their lives and the children will never see that parent again.

The use of aversion therapy to unconsciously alter intimate personal identity and autonomy of thought and polyvagal therapy (a form of brain stimulus outside of the subject's conscious control) are acts of autocratic control used to suppress or distort evidence of crimes by obliterating the consciousness of crimes committed. The silencing of child victims through the use of unmonitored, unlicensed programs, Is nothing less than massive malpractice.

These third-world war prisoner tactics, these threats, intimidation, defamation of the protective parents, manipulation, lies, and gaslighting will be supplemented by several other manipulations. Children are to have no contact with the outside world, no electronics, no television, and no other people in their lives, especially not those who believed their cries for help. The accused parent—even one accused of sexual abuse—will be allowed physical contact, touching, rubbing, and feeling the child who has rejected them, in order to desensitize the child to physical contact with the alleged abuser.

The internal strength of each child will determine the success or failure of this model of modern warfare, this heinous assault on the minds, bodies, and spirits of the most vulnerable. Reports from the survivors of these reunification programs anecdotally describe tightly regimented daily routines, intensely limited contact, use of film, reading material, and hypnotic techniques to shape thoughts and attitudes, and use of forms of punitive behavior modification and thought control.

Children separated from the parents who sought to protect them are now isolated with their abuser and sent to schools where only the now custodial parent has any contact or communication. The narrative to all who surround the child is that the parent from whom these children have been "rescued" is crazy, and possibly the children are crazy too and may have to be sent to psychiatric hospitals.

"Reunification" programs are put in place to seek to ensure the direction of custody from a protective parent into the hands of those who will silence and suppress any form of free speech or communication with a rescuing outside world. Forcing isolation of a child, and prohibiting all contact with anyone other than an accused abuser constitutes a new level of unconscionable child abuse.

"Reunification therapy" is its own new kind of coercive management horror.

Chapter 15

But What About the Children's Testimony?

Years before I came to know of juvenile, dependency, and family court corruption, I knew that children must be seen, heard, and believed, or they will disappear.

Children speak what they have seen, heard, and experienced. But they are not believed. In the context of crimes against children, hidden, suppressed, and denied, "do not believe your lying eyes" has reached a new level.

Crimes are brought to court, testified to, with evidence provided, and with multiple credible witnesses. But in family court, the argument has become that the victim "misperceived, misunderstood what took place," if anything took place at all. Even when children give clear testimony of abuse, the "other parent" is accused of "coaching," which is nearly impossible to do convincingly with a child. "Herding cats" is the phrase I use to describe attempting to get a child to impart a desired narrative.

The children, disbelieved by the very authorities who have sworn to protect them, to act in their "best interest," are sent off to live with their abuser. These children have a choice: adapt to their surroundings, become people far different from whom they were destined to be, or die.

The path to rescue for too many of these children does not come quickly enough to mitigate the suffering they endure, and "treatment" is not directed to the benefit of the child, but to the cover-up of the crimes.

Children do not vote. Children do not pay taxes. Children cannot organize to protest against their abusers. Children are commodities, at the bidding of whoever is in control.

Even the littlest ones can express themselves, though, by their moods and behavior. When they are cheerful and playful at one moment, then moody, angry, and withdrawn, what was it that distressed them? When allowed to express themselves, they do, and wittingly or unwittingly, they tend to tell the truth.

One little one of about four told her friends that she sometimes did babyish things like sucking her thumb and wanting her blanket with her. She asked the assembled toddlers how they stopped doing these "babyish" things, imagining that they had stopped. Then she went on to describe to them how she had been punished by her father, who took her blanket and stuffed toys and locked her in the garage.

She and her parents lived in the most beautiful fairytale-like home. Her fairy princess room would never have revealed the secrets she shared that day.

A young teen paced the hallways of a psychiatric unit for teens considered to be chronically ill, or simply untreatable. She stared in a trance, moving as if in a goose-stepping march, stating over and over again, "I am dead. I am dead." As inquiry progressed, a story unfolded of a gruesome, brutal, spontaneous assault that resulted in the murder of her little brother before her eyes. It appeared that other child members had also disappeared, but no investigation was made until this child's psychosis began to resolve and the mystery was pursued by police, and the evidence of crimes was uncovered.

Children must be seen, heard, and believed, or else they will disappear.

Within the context of a family relationship, violence against children and abuse of children is often minimized. But the damage to the child's psyche is not minimized.

Courts fail to come to grips with the reality that home and family are the nests for the most primitive and dangerous crimes, because power, wealth, and control combine with dependency, neediness, and vulnerability. In family court, it is more likely that a child will be seriously maimed, injured, or murdered, than that their complaints will be honestly addressed.

The child who reacts with rejection and or a host of other "negative" reactions to an abusing, destructive parent, instead of being viewed as exhibiting a normal, healthy, appropriate reaction to a situation of personal harm and danger is treated as an empty vessel to be directed by an opposing force. If the child asserts an independent will, in opposition to the authority demanding association with the rejected party, that child may find themselves demeaned, ridiculed, and subject to harsh punishment. That punishment, meant to ensure a coerced outcome, includes confinement, isolation, and interment. That confinement, under court order, may include a juvenile detention program, psychiatric hospital, or the "reunification program."

The honest, forthright statements of children in their own words, in their terms, are unmistakable. They are clear to those who listen and for those who are not engaged as hired guns to protect bad acts through manipulation, alteration of data, and misinterpretation of technical, clinical material.

Those who seek to remove children as witnesses to crimes or victims of crimes, seek to maintain their subjects in isolation, under control, and under threat of ongoing punishment to the subject child. When such children attempt to flee or seek help from within the captive environment, methods to pursue and capture children through the FBI, Amber Alert system, or local police signals known as Silver Alerts create major obstacles and dangers for children and parents seeking escape from a well-organized abuser. Organizations such as The Foundation for Missing and Exploited Children accept alerts indiscriminately without reliable vetting so that, in the direct experience with FCVFC clients, perpetrators of harm to children are active reporters on this site seeking to track down victims fleeing from the abuser hunting the victim with the support of the public.

The children in these situations are broken and confused. They cannot trust others and have great difficulty making decisions or even trusting their own decisions. Unless survivors of court-initiated trauma and terror receive excellent therapy as adults, their stories will remain hidden.

Caring, loving parents would not willingly, knowingly subject their children to this fully manipulated out-of-control circus referred to by the FCVFC as a criminal enterprise. This enterprise is motivated by immobilizing fear generated by their lawyers and advisors. Children in family courts have no voices, and apparently societal forces would have it no other way. But children must be seen, heard, and believed, or else they will disappear.

And they are disappearing. The violations within each case and the consequences to litigants must be confronted, litigated, and prosecuted, both civilly and criminally, with damages consequences to perpetrators of harm, beginning with judges and moving through the phalanx of culpable officers of the courts.

Chapter 16

Who Are Those Abusive Court Actors?

The covenant of good faith underlies the basis of any legal system, as the public places faith in their elected or appointed representatives. The public agrees to be bound by the judgments and findings of those authorities elected or appointed by trusted members of the community.

But the preceding chapters have laid out the true state of affairs. This is not only deplorable but devastating as to the societal consequences wrought by acts of calumny, selfishness, greed, and psychopathy, all in the name of "justice." The overreach of judicial authority, when driven by mendacious moves related to extensive character and psychological depravity, poses an acute threat to the core of a democratic society, the family.

Excellent books and articles rail against inequities, cruelty, and damages in the home, but many of those who read these books are also witnesses to the travesty of the family courts. Experts on cruelty in the home must also see the cruelty of court actors in the family courts.

The abuser script

Whether the partner abuser is a man or a woman, the abuser script reads, "My partner is crazy, my partner has a very serious mental illness, saying these awful things about me, convincing the kids to lie and distort things. The children must be protected for their welfare, the children must be in therapy, the partner must be in therapy and cannot see the kids until they admit to their lies and get help for their mental illness."

Charm, attractiveness, and glibness of speech are used to engage the sympathy of friends, family, and neighbors: "This poor guy/girl is saddled with that crazy wife/husband and those awful, selfish, unappreciative kids."

Once this script arrives in family court, it immediately reaches a receptive and willing crew of producers and actors. This script will receive a production team, a cast, a performance, an execution plan, and a closing act, which ends with removing vulnerable children from protective parents and removing them into the hands of abusers.

Another critical aspect of the script to justify aberrant behavior, abuse, or even addiction is accusing the innocent spouse. "My spouse drove me to drink and caused me to become an alcoholic. "My spouse drove me to have sex with my child." (Chapter 10 highlights some quotations from Richard Gardner in which he indicates this as a valid excuse.)

The main character: the psychopathic judge

Family court judges used to be known for having the disposition to provide flexibility and reasonableness, to

CHAPTER 16

take off their black robes and talk with children about their thoughts and feelings, on camera in their offices. Flexibility, compassion, and interest in hearing from all parties are still factored into the evaluation of custody decisions in most courts.

But the amiable atmosphere of good judges seeking to engage in the reasonable, equitable settlement was an ebbing practice, and the tsunami, the all-consuming appetite for the new expeditious settlement of cases through the mesmerizing concept of "parental alienation" was in its inception.

Soon it would overtake the imagination and the marketing mechanisms of legal practitioners, who saw all the possibilities it offered for the growth of cottage industries and conveyor-belt processes for litigating a whole new branch of law, manufactured as high-conflict custody litigation.

Chapter 13 described in brief the bias we see in family court judges. But in many cases, "bias" is the gentlest word I can find.

In family court, the judge wields the power to destroy lives. There is no jury determining guilt or innocence; it is the judge alone who will make the declaration of how fit you are as a parent, which parent will be the ultimate custodian of the children, how the bills are to be paid, and more.

Family court judges have the incomprehensibly horrific ability to make entire families disappear—to take happy, thriving, loving children and turn them into something that is not only a shadow of themselves, but something unable to be reclaimed as per the damage inflicted. I call the judge who sends children to certain abuse, trauma, and destruction, the "family annihilator."

This judge may have a personality disorder similar to that of the abusers to whom they are sentencing the children. They share many of the same character-disordered traits as the perverts and pathologically abusive characters against whom the protective parent is seeking protection.

When a protective parent brings to the court evidence of heinous crimes involving physical, sexual, and emotional abuse that will traumatize, demoralize, and cripple children, and a judge then transfers custody of the children to the criminal, I see the character and psychological of these judges as reflections of the monsters that they appear to admire.

I see traits of narcissistic personality disorder in both: controlling, manipulative, always correct, innocent of any wrongdoing, always an authority that must be obeyed, with an intense dislike or even hatred of the protective parent. Loss of control produces the shame of fear and abandonment, an emotion most despised. Thus, the disgust with which the protective parent is viewed and the determination to ever maintain absolute control.

The FCVFC writes about family court judges who are even known to have presided over cases that involve murders and suicides, of children and/or spouses. Yet they go without public commentary or notice. The public doesn't even blink.

Male and female judges are indistinguishable as to their level of cruelty. What is clear is the entitlement they feel to do as they please and the lack of consequence for the harm they have caused. We see a pattern of greater and greater brazen behavior, arrogance, and risk-taking on the part of both male and female judges and their cohorts. Sua sponte and IPSE Dixit Judicial Orders ("of the moment," "because I say so" orders) are frequently implemented by power-hungry judges engaged in unlawful, spontaneous custody transfers.

For these judges, there is no thought or option to ever engage in restorative justice. No, the depth and breadth of their sense of entitlement appear to be fixed and immovable. Over and over, day after day, they are faced with the pleadings and even hysterics of children who beg not to go to their abusers. But they are never seen to budge from their cruel, inhumane orders, even when those orders have resulted in murders and/or suicides.

But however biased and abusive a judge may be, however much he or she may violate due process, it is still very difficult to remove a judge from a case. These attempts are often met by paroxysms of retaliation in the form of contempt charges that include massive legal fee assignments, jail, and further isolation from the children.

Our experience has been that judges will even lie for judges as cases move from family court to federal court. Judicial peers who are offended by complaints against their colleagues support the crimes reported to judicial review boards and beyond by altering the scripts, the facts, and the interpretations of the law, in order to protect judicial offenders. Appeals court judges do the same, following the same manipulation and code of loyalty, not to the law, but to those who betray the fatal flaw in the law: corrupt officers of the court.

Elected and appointed judges have become a class of anointed judges who engage in the unprecedented practice of transferring children of all ages into the hands of abusers. And this, regardless of how venal are the crimes against children, articulated and substantiated by objective evidence. All abuse allegations are denied, evidence suppressed, and witnesses intimidated and threatened as a matter of course. The abuse of process has come to be recognized via the issuance of contempt charges to unlawfully retaliate against those who engage in the legal process in an attempt to protect vulnerable children.

Introducing the sycophants

The family court judge does not work in isolation. Those life-altering, life-destroying decisions are made with the help of other court actors. These judges surround themselves with sycophantic supporters who are well-educated and professionally accomplished. Though the credentials and accomplishments of the anointed/appointed may not be as significant or credible as they superficially appear to be, the coterie of "talent" around the judge are trusted supporters, politically astute, who deliver the intuitively understood outcomes desired by the judge and other seemingly credible, court-appointed authorities of the court stage.

In the family courts, lawyers, guardians ad litem, and court-appointed psychological evaluators and therapists have joined together to become threats to intellectually competent, psychologically compos mentis, moral, ethical society. Thus, the court process has grown into an autocratic, criminal process laying waste to a vast section of the population.

Court actors who have been appointed by judges enjoy qualified immunity and live under the illusion of immunity from prosecution. They act with reckless abandon. They engage in practices of racketeering, witness intimidation, and suppression of evidence. These court actors in their professional roles delegitimize legitimate complaints. They consolidate gains by isolating children from their protectors, breaking their spirits, and deepening their despair for hopes of rescue.

In addition to the local cabal of lawyers and associated professionals of the family courts, another entirely corrupt agency has arisen, bloated with money and power, the so-called "Child Protective Services." This agency has been known to strike fear into the hearts of those who must interface with them.

Known for their practices of hiring ill-trained staff and having a reputation as acting more like thugs and enforcers than as child protective officers, they can remove children at will and maintain them in situations where they may be irreparably harmed.

CPS has layers and layers of bureaucracy—and at every level, lawyers—to enforce and protect the installed abusers, who then have a license to act on any primal instinct which they may wish.

The population of judges and their minions who cooperate and contract to pervert an entire system of juvenile justice is propagating to cover the entire American landscape.

The "criminal" attorney and the "team" you never knew you hired

The client with guilty secrets to hide knows he needs a "criminal" attorney, an attorney who is by penchant and character a criminal, one willing to bend, stretch, and manipulate the law and the litigation process.

Further, the "criminal" attorney/attorney who is a criminal can maintain a level of oblivion, disregard, deniable ignorance, and lack of accountability when it comes to the harm enacted on innocents, with laser focus and energy to pursue a strategy that will exonerate his or her client while indelibly and massively harming others.

The outcome of high-net-worth cases is predetermined based on the financial disclosure statement and how much, or who has more money to drive the outcome, bought and sold before anyone has produced one line of evidence that will be ignored and discredited, combated with some pre fixe scheme. Such was the scenario played out by a multi-millionaire (or billionaire) family whose multiple members were afflicted with the acute diseases of alcohol and drug addiction, as the generations of wealth were based on importing and shipping alcoholic products across the USA and the world, that resulted in the deaths and personal destruction of multiple family members.

The lie that shapes the divorce narrative

The connected attorney develops the "team" of predator professionals, consisting of the guardian ad litem or best interest attorney or attorney for the children, the evaluator, and therapists of various sorts. It is the team that protective parents never knew they hired.

The connected lawyer with the connected team makes contact with the connected judge and connected "experts," predator professionals who set the narrative. He or she then begins the high-conflict custody racketeering game that characterizes the nature of abuse-associated custody litigation across the country. Like a team of dogs in the Alaskan Iditarod, the connected lawyer will engage in an orchestrated process, one which the naïve litigant will eventually come to recognize as illegal and lethal.

In Howard County, Maryland, a certain team frequently worked together on multiple cases. One worked as the client's attorney, the other as a guardian ad litem (Alyssa Cummins and Christopher Rand, usually accompanied by psychologist Paul Berman). They assembled further associates: the therapists for the family, one for the mother, one for the father, and one for the children. Because of the number of appointments for everyone, a treatment coordinator was also needed, who called balls and strikes on who was doing what to whom and when.

This Howard County, Maryland, the team perfected the protocol of "the team that the targeted client never knew they hired." This team, which performed like the perfectly coordinated Radio City Rockettes, knocked off case after case, transferring children who were the subjects of lies and liars, abusers and vengeful, spiteful spouses who hated their spouses more than they even began to care for their children. The client with money to burn and a passion to win at all costs would win, as the costs were driven into the multi-hundreds of thousands of dollars, often spent on the services of inept attorneys, with the liberties of family court judges who pushed unlikely defenses through, based on judicial discretion.[73]

The ability to mesmerize listeners with a soap-opera-like saga, where trials become theatrical productions—this is a dynamic that we see as central to these high-conflict

---

[73] Jill Jones Soderman, "A Case for Investigation: A Call to Action," The Foundation for Child Victims of the Family Courts, https://fcvfc.org/2019/08/20/a-case-for-investigation-a-call-to-action-ellicott-city

litigations. Evidence, however compelling, may have caused judges, with tears in their eyes, to ignore evidence and transfer suffering, devastated children into not only the sole custody, but into the solid isolation of an abuser with secrets to hide. As our experience and expertise have demonstrated, the pre-fixe element of outcomes is an inescapable conclusion when one parses the elements of the case as was demonstrated by one, among many Howard County, Maryland, cases.

A father of three pre-teen children was faced with the catastrophic consequences of his wife's alcohol addiction, the onset of approximately ten years into their marriage. Following seven failed hospitalizations in various luxurious alcohol treatment facilities, car accidents, CPS investigation involvement for endangering the children, the marriage headed for divorce.

The father had a rather sterling history of character, decency, reliability, and devotion to family and community. He had no apparent family or personal history of mental illness or addiction. He was wealthy in his own right and supported his family in a very comfortable lifestyle. He loved his wife and children and did not want a divorce. His wife was the genetic recipient of multiple generations of family members who suffered from the disease of alcoholism and denial. Denial of the tragedies that haunted the generations was enforced by the wealth that expunged criminal charges and gave treatment in luxurious, confidentially protected treatment facilities. However the death by a drug overdose of a young relative of the wife's family precipitated profiles and news coverage.

The demand for the specter of addiction and mental illness to be eliminated from the picture meant erasing the presence of the wife's alcoholism because her alcoholism caused her to act in ways that required some oversight for the protection of the children. The wife's family, with personal generational wealth, demanded that the alcoholism be "erased." The legal team, enforced by hired gun prevaricators, developed the false narrative that the husband drove her to drink, the husband was secretly violent, controlling, and abusive. The secret was so well kept that literally no one, including—or shall we say, especially—the children knew anything about it and so, the legal team, which included the attorney for the father, became witnesses against their own client. The attorney for the client provided sworn testimony that she herself had been or at least felt threatened. She brought a violence charge against her client that caused her to be a witness in the case against her own client, a witness to an event that the client could prove never occurred but was never provided a venue to present such evidence.

Predetermined outcomes to cases driven by power and money, defined by the attorney with the wealthiest client, with culpability to hide, turns the attorney for the protective parent—whom one would have thought would be an advocate—into another member of the "team" for the adversary with secrets to hide and a goal they insist upon achieving.

Let us note that though this story ended in defeat, it did not need to. This client's next attorney, excellent and skilled though he was, refused to deal with the core criminality and venality of the case. He ignored the psychological factors of the adversary to a straightforward, not very complex, parent. The complex pathology and secrets to hide, the hubris, and the need to exert control of the family myth, were not taken into proper consideration. He "missed" the proper needed interventions. This new attorney was sure that his superb legal arguments would win over the judge, who was intrigued, engaged, and responsive to his many legal tactics and interventions, which generated hundreds of thousands of dollars in legal fees for all dimensions of the case. The trial dragged on and resembled something more of a World Wrestling Entertainment match than a legitimate trial, with superstar lawyers and psychological interventionists. A trial that should have taken weeks dragged on for approximately one year, and costs on both sides of the aisle exceeded half a million dollars.

The protective parent's lawyer

Most often, the divorce process is set off by the partner in control of marital assets and most able to take independent, unrestrained action. The naïve spouse, compelled to take action, hires a seemingly logical, reasonable expert.

If you have brought forward evidence that your child experienced sexual, physical, or emotional abuse at the hands of the other parent, you may have already learned that these charges will be fiercely, ferociously contested by the court. The protective parent will rapidly be accused of being a "parent alienator," a la Gardner protocol, which states that (all) accusations of sexual abuse are false and must be held as a suspect, as that parent is driven by spite and malice to create an advantage against an innocent partner. The child is deemed to have been abused by the accuser of false claims, by dint of having been manipulated, brainwashed, or induced into making false statements against a parent who is elevated to the level of the better parent. The abuser parent is depicted as being "strict," or imposing discipline, and the child is just "spoiled" and seeking to be with the indulgent parent. This sua sponte fairytale blossoms despite clear evidence that the "spoiled brat "child is suicidal, cutting, or starving themselves, and a one-time stellar functioning on multiple fronts is replaced with failing grades, missing school, and clear symptoms of acute anxiety. Psychiatric medications and behavioral treatment are prescribed to assist the child in functionally "handling" their anxiety. *Breathe, try to understand that whatever you think is going on—is not happening and your "interpretation of events" are thoughts that have been communicated by your (offending) parent and you might think about the situation as …. such and so…. and you might discuss with your (parent) what you are feeling.*

A girl of 12 was made to dress in front of her father each morning as she was getting ready for school. She was directed to stand before her father in her underwear so that he could adjust her breasts in her bra. She described closing her eyes as she stood before him, but she could not avoid the noises of his masturbating as he was "adjusting her breasts in her bra." When the distraught child informed teachers and guidance counselors at her Jewish school, their initial outrage and attempts to help her faded as the father and his lawyers threatened to sue the school and file grievances against their licenses. The abuser father, who gained full custody of the child, removed her from her Jewish religious school and transferred her to a Catholic school.

The "team," court-appointed to review, share, comment upon, and discuss the protective parent's past, present, and future, delivers the court-ordered new regimen with scripts for how, or if, the protective parent can interact with the children at all. The "treatment team" will order the "offending" parent into "treatment" to teach how to speak to the child, and to encourage the "relationship" with the parent who has been credibly and properly accused of abuse. The court / "treatment team" will supervise visits when such visits are deemed permissible, meaning that the parent has fully altered their communication and behavior.

The protective parent will most likely find that their lawyer, who was trusted to help protect the children, is working in lockstep with the rest of the team in order to protect the personal identity and image of the blamelessness of the abuser, who has rapidly gained custody of the children who are no longer able to have any communication with the protective parent. The child's technology is removed, and the school is notified that the offending parent can have no contact with or information about any aspect of the child's school functioning or academic performance.

Lawyers for the protective parent do not want to be subject to punishment that can be meted out by the judge—after all, they have a career to consider. So the position of the lawyer is to feign ignorance or blame the client, because just as the judge is acting exclusively for their own benefit and gratification, so ultimately is the protective parent's lawyer, whose lucrative income is dependent on "winning" cases in the jurisdiction in which licensed.

These attorneys can be noisy in their ineffectual displays of courtroom drama, but their efforts are meaningless, or even harmful. Your attorney may urge you to compromise so that the case can move smoothly through the court. This compromise may look like dropping the protective order you worked so hard to have filed (in the name of appearing reasonable and operating with goodwill), allowing the children to have limited contact with the abuser again, and even retracting the accusations of sexual abuse. Arguments are made that "it only happened once," "so and so is in treatment," "the children are in treatment…" The result of these nonsense arguments is that the children can be dead and the abuser can be in jail, or the children are severely traumatized and emotionally harmed over the entire course of their lives, injured throughout the full life course of development, and impacting generations to come.

Instead of acting in the best interest of their clients, these attorneys have often acted in lockstep with the illegal, eviscerating directives of the court, moving the children into the custody of an abuser, stifling communications of abuse, and maximizing the flow of reliable child support. Your lawyer becomes your adversary's collegial teammate, supporting the agenda of the adversary from whom you were trying to separate and protect your children.

Your attorney expresses no remorse, only blaming you, under the control of the abjectly characterologically deranged judge, with whom the lawyer's role and strategy are linked and driven. Detailed descriptions of judges whose hubris, ignorance, disrespect, and disregard for the law and the welfare of the community the judge was sworn to serve are on bold display in the articles that populate the FCVFC website. These descriptions can also be found in the panoply of social media and news articles that rail over the grossly underreported deaths by murder and suicide of innocent, vulnerable children.

The goal to bring children into the custody of the person from whom the protective parent was trying to protect them—with clear evidence, though suppressed—is nothing less than a despicable, immoral criminal act. Crimes against children and innocent protective parents must be recognized as crimes, as criminal acts are being committed by court actors and attendant professionals who act as enforcers of illegitimate court orders and directives.

Those families who live under the delusion that the U.S. family, dependency, and juvenile court systems function as legitimate institutions are in acute danger. The court systems and government agencies that control the administration of justice and protection of children must be recognized as operating as criminal enterprises driven by profit motives, creating revenue streams through child support to the states, while court actors are driven by profit motives, while abusers seek to profit from their crimes.

Family members who elude prosecution for crimes for which they would have been immediately pursued if the crime was not taking place in the context of marriage and family are now given shade by a court system primed by the Gardner spurious narrative and the cottage industry spawned by a court system that has learned to propagate litigation.

Evaluators and their evaluations

The FCVFC is fully familiar with the cast of psychopathic predators who parade as licensed professionals. They are equal opportunity abusers who have no bias in taking money from men or women to slowly, painfully exsanguinate the lifeblood out of their victim—men, women, and children—probably separating platelets from other blood products for the highest rate of return.

When facts and reality become malleable factors, subject to conjecture, argument, hearsay, and speculation, the vacuum created in the space where facts and reality are up for grabs is a space filled by power, money, and criminal activity, able to be organized, coordinated and systematized.

For example, in order to verify whether or not you are a fit parent, the family court has resorted to the "psychological evaluation" given by an "evaluator."

The evaluator is a court-appointed psychologist, appointed from the list of court-approved experts. The litigant is not asked about this but is simply informed. You will have to do your own research to find out any credentials and reputation, but if you do not like what you find, it will make no difference to the court. In some cases, the court-appointed agent is assigned and the client is not even provided the name or credentials of the person who now has considerable authority over their lives.

This "expert" will use proprietary testing to make confidential assessments of each litigant and the children, as to mental state, character, and the veracity of statements. Then this person will make a recommendation as to custody, visitation, therapy, and even medication recommendations. The judge will most often listen to and follow those recommendations.

You will not be allowed to question the interpretation of the data. In many courts, you will not even know what it is, because it is kept confidential, even from you and your representatives.

These reports include the evaluator's subjective impressions, judgments, and comments about a wide range of subjects including home and lifestyle. The evaluator is allowed to roam and graze on the internal and external components of their subjects' lives.

The same soft-science, hearsay-filled, unverified, speculative, non-evidence-based ruminations of psychological evaluators that were once viewed with skepticism, are now elevated to determine the course of the lives of individuals for years extending beyond the term of the divorce and custody decision. The judicial role in many cases has become subservient to this clinical assessment. Evaluators are non-judicial personnel, often of questionable academic rigor and qualifications for the tasks assigned, yet they are handed the keys to the kingdom of making fundamental assessments and determinations regarding credibility and evidentiary determinations.

Evaluators, acting in place of law enforcement, forensic science, best interest, and best practices are replacing the fact-finding functions of the judge, as judges fully predicate their decision-making function to the evaluation report and associated recommendations.

The reports are written by judicial order and with judicial authority and are granted qualified immunity from any accountability concerning lawsuits. The authors of these life-altering reports have nothing to lose.

The "therapists" and the documents

Court authorities protected by qualified immunity, judges, lawyers for plaintiffs and defendants, and lawyers for children, all compose the team who coerce desperate parents into engaging in a process of so-called therapy.

Desperate parents in fear of being held in contempt of court are forced to compel children into brutal interviews with callous and obtuse interviewers who call themselves therapists. Children are forced to articulate repressed experiences, to justify and explain their fears, only to be told to "ignore their feelings," to push them down, to work around them—as if these words had meaning beyond the push to insanity, as madness becomes the psyche's only nurse.

The performance drama

At the onset of the litigation process, there would be no reason to suspect foul play. But you have entered the world of kabuki dance, where like kabuki syndrome, all systems are abnormal.

As you try to explain your children's fear, terror, and abuse at the hands of the predator you wish to evade for yourself and the children, you will find to your horror that the tables are being turned and you have become the person under suspicion. The rug is pulled out from under you, and the children are suddenly, inexplicably, thrown back into the custody of the abuser.

You may begin to feel that you are insane as you cannot believe that the statements of your children, the evidence of abuse you had until moments before, when you viewed such evidence compelling and clear beyond any doubt, has suddenly thrown you into a position of suspicion, doubt, and ridicule.

You may lose control of the narrative that guides the complaint and may even lose control of all facts and evidence that support the case. This is why we emphasize over and over that evidence must be protected, validated, authenticated, and never lost sight of. These cases must be managed with an intense focus on protecting facts in the complaint and protecting the subject child or children.

You will be marched through the gauntlet of meaningless hearings meant to extract fees from you, as you grasp at every opportunity to be in contact with your children, just as the abuser is taking advantage of every opportunity to withhold child contact.

The defamation process begins with a referral from the list of court-approved psychological practitioners whom the court can be assured is familiar with whatever types of highly toxic diagnoses to be assigned to destroy the protective parent's career, relationships with friends and family, and sense of self.

You have been taking action to make things better. To your great shock and dismay, you suddenly find yourself disenfranchised from every single aspect of your life, in the grip of a malevolent presence. You find yourself in the position of being a puppet whose strings are being pulled as you become a character in a deadly Punch and Judy show, subject to the whims and merciless indiscretions of a cruel presence known only to those who have experienced it, the family court cabal, the racketeering crew, the mob boss judge who is impervious, unmoved and largely indifferent to your child's and your own pleas. If you do not display utter obsequious obeisance at all times, the cold indifference will give way to pure retaliatory rage.

Suddenly, you find that you must force yourself and your children to engage positively with a person who caused harm and trauma as those events are redefined and re-imagined, normalized, and the depth of depravity diminished or denied.

Part of the performance drama is the secreted presence of confidential, sealed documents. The protective parent rarely if ever has access to these documents easily in reach of the parent who is awarded custody. Those who will take the time to read these court documents, evaluations, police reports, affidavits, etc., will find that these documents support the claims of abuse.

Plot synopsis

The naïve seeker of justice appeals for relief from crimes, spouting the truisms of scholarly articles on domestic violence and coercive control as well as "The Law."

But the overseers of justice are themselves the doppelgangers, mirror images by character and deeds, of the original criminal. They too commit their well-established crimes of collusion, fraud, perjury, and so on and on and on.

So, the seekers of justice—the protective parent, along with the victim child—are left helpless and at the mercy of kangaroo courts and predatory attorneys whose financial incentives are supported by the state, in the form of child support incentives, as well as by judges whose back-channel benefits must be examined per case, per judge.

The Kafkaesque court proceedings, which one might liken to those of Torquemada of the Spanish Inquisition, seeking out heretics, further injected with Marquis de Sade sadism and the plot of Shades of Grey, accurately describe the uniform state of custody litigation in courts across the United States.

United in a perverse and cruel form of execution of innocents, the U.S. courts are engaged in a form of genocide hiding in plain sight and in full view of a passive, placid public, moving toward the decimation of society's most valuable and critical asset: our children.

It will be small comfort to learn that the same scene, the same script, is played out in every state in the Union, in every family courtroom in the country.

An example comes in the form of a case before a much-discussed judge, Jane K. Grossman of Connecticut. Police were called by FCVFC forensic expert staff to investigate a charge of child sexual assault, not the first assault reported. The police then took the very clear and credible statement of the child.

In police files there already existed nude pictures of two little toddler boys standing with their grandfather on the front lawn of his home. The grandfather, known to have sexually assaulted his son throughout his son's life, was facing the camera, holding one grandson's penis in his hand while the other child stared wide-eyed at the scene. Police reports had been filed regarding both father and son for sexual assaults on the two boys and their baby sister, who is deaf and speech impaired.

The police officers detailed the report and contacted DCF in Connecticut, who ordered the children removed from the father's home to the home of the grandfather, only yards away from his son's home. The court hearing that ensued before Judge Jane K. Grossman proceeded to file multiple charges against the mother, transfer full custody to the father, and allow no contact between the mother and her three young children. Further punitive actions enacted by Judge Jane K. Grossman are documented in the transcripts of this case and others where children were subject to multiple forms of horrendous abuse.

CHAPTER 16

Heinous acts of cruelty are routinely excused and exonerated by Judge Jane K. Grossman, whose animus and venal display of hatred of the mothers/reporters in these cases is always in full display. Judge Grossman also displays naked hostility toward anyone who defends the clear object of her biased directives.

Attorney Nickola Cunha, an attorney advocate for many controversial cases in Connecticut, served as a sacrificial lamb to provide a chilling message to any lawyer who seeks to mount a defense for a litigant marked for Judge Jane Grossman's campaign of vengeance, as an instant lifetime removal of this attorney's legal license was pursued in the course of a heated trial that took place in New Haven, Connecticut in 2020 and 2021.

DCF in Connecticut requested a full forensic evaluation of the children, but as the father has custody of the three children with all medical, legal, and educational decision-making and control, he refused the forensic evaluation, without which DCF felt they could not move forward with abuse charges against the father, who was reported by the FCVFC for sexual assault.

The only good news in the case to date is that our client is strong, brilliant, and courageous and allowing the FCVFC to take all necessary actions to litigate, prosecute, and pursue damages against ALL participants in the multiple forms of abuse visited on these children. But why should these children be forced to suffer through the time it is taking to pursue their protection, which is being stonewalled by a judge who has proven herself to be a psychopathic predator and abuser of the lofty position that she holds?[74]

---

[74] See more at "Judges as Family Annihilators," The Foundation for Child Victims of the Family Courts, September 12, 2022, https://fcvfc.org/2022/09/12/judges-as-family-annihilators.

The lawyers, who know their places and their lines, routinely line up their clients like frogs in water, turning up the heat as the client tries to understand what's happening. Then the water reaches the boiling point: The court and associated minions will teach you what it is to lose your autonomy as well as any sense of justice.

Lawyers that you thought were fighting for the children will inform you that if you do not do as directed, you will find yourself in jail and your children expedited into the custody of their abuser. In effect, your civil rights, such as your first amendment right to free speech, and the right to association and representation, are abrogated, violated, and decimated.

You will then be offered the glimmer of hope—if all the rules are followed—of supervised visitation, with supervisors chosen by the legal team and vested by the judge with the right to control the narrative. The protective parent is forced into the position of cooperating with the abuse and ultimate destruction of their child.

Chapter 17

What's Going on Behind the Scenes in Family Court

Entry of a protocol to defend pedophiles, psychopaths, and the mentally ill who suddenly became deserving of the largesse offered by parenthood in the form of marital assets and child support opened a class of paying parties that shifted the burden of parental fitness and best interest parameters to the one who will pay the most money for easy, available access to children.

In the family courts, litigants find themselves enmeshed in a system that is ultimately dedicated to the re-allotment of family wealth. Exactly how do the forces promoting this type of organized, prefix litigation strategy insure payment for this immensely expensive plan of action?

Follow the money

The study of Title IV-D agencies for each of the 50 states defines the incentives of state child support guidelines that pull federal funds to feed state programs, which are destroying the lives of millions of children.

Do not let anyone tell you otherwise! Child support guidelines and the funding Title IV-D must be studied for each case in order to attempt to deal with underlying motives and interventions and to confront any suspected corruption, including payments to court-appointed so-called experts.

The psychological evaluator has access to intimate personal medical, educational, psychiatric, and court records. The court team has access to your case information statement, your taxes, your bank statements, and your credit reports. The bottom line is that your income and assets become their fees—short-term, interim, and long-term.

This scheme of litigation is set to defraud family court litigants out of their funds, making them incapable of protecting their children. Often the scheme begins before the parent even sets foot in court, with early assessment being made as to who gets what and for how much. No need to evaluate evidence in court when these bottom-line decisions can be established with the first look at the Financial Case Information Statement.

The Financial Case Information Statement for litigants becomes the budget for the extended evaluation and litigation process, involving the team you have been tasked with having to hire and support.

The process about to unfold will then absorb every waking moment of the party's and children's lives, under court order and threat of contempt hearings.

Sudden judicial orders freeze the funds of the protective parent (usually not the funds of the accused abuser) and even children's financial accounts. Property owned by the protective parent is suddenly confiscated on spurious terms without contest.

CHAPTER 17

Often, a judge who knows in advance of proceedings what needs to be hidden will issue gag orders for the protective parent and have files sealed from prying eyes.

The false narrative protecting abusers of children is headed by the attorney whose larger-than-normal retainer and fees mirror the larger-than-normal retainer and fees of each of the other court actors, whose bills go on and on and on.

The expenditure of larger than normal fees for an array of experts with questionable credentials, questionable reputations is part of the arsenal deployed by a parent with bad acts to hide and funds to invest for their reputation and asset protection.

The experts that make up the "custody team" are part of an approved court list of those who produce predictable outcomes. Their licenses are protected from lawsuits by qualified immunity and protected from licensing board review because the court will not share court files with licensing boards (confidential court testimony).

Those who would sue them have had their reputations damaged by smear campaigns inside and outside of the court litigation.

Hiring a family court lawyer can cost 25, 50, or 75 thousand dollars. Then they must have accouterments: therapists for all parties, an individual therapist and a family therapist, as well as a guardian ad litem, along with an assortment of evaluators for testing.

The protective parents thought they were paying for defenders. They had no idea that the outcome had been decided before they began.

The court actors provide window dressing and set the stage for the judicial performance that delivers helpless, hapless families from farm to market, where a division of marital assets, child support, and child support enforcement are the real targets of judicial rulings that seek the ultimate reward: financial remuneration shared with colleagues and then reaching out to government agencies by funding programs which involve the police, CPS, criminal justice, and politician's campaigns.

It is a racketeering process

Racketeering is an organized scheme to extract illegal profits. In family court, the elements of racketeering are confirmed by looking at the collateral contacts and interlocking associations of court actors as to business and professional connections. Racketeering partners support, validate, and insulate each other. They provide their reputation repair services as they refer clients to each other and support each other's work and opinions, as one speaks the lies and the others swear to the lies.

Another criterion for racketeering is established when we see referrals to resources at a stage in the case where such a referral could not have been anticipated.

We know that racketeering is in progress when we see the lines of communication established for children to be sent to "reunification" programs before a court has whispered the dreaded sentence associated with "parental alienation." Before any orders from the court to remove children from protective parents into the hands of their abusers, those predator professionals have established the links to "reunification programs" to continue the pipeline of fees from desperate parents and referral fees to the pipeline feeders.

We see the conscious, coordinated efforts of a team of professionals, working together toward a conscious, malicious goal to promote a false narrative that exclusively benefits one side of a litigation proceeding, by stacking the evidence in favor of that side. The narrative promoted is unsubstantiated, and not supported by facts or the submission of proper evidence. The elements of coercion, control, confabulation, and manipulation exist to the point that clients find that their attorneys are contributing to their demise by providing information and evidence against them in a court of law, to benefit and support the case of their adversary.

These manipulated proceedings give evidence of being the means to extract huge amounts of money. They bury facts and truth under piles of paper. They allow inserted "facts" placed by judicial commentary and meanderings to fill loopholes the judge knows may be brought up in appeal.

This funding subsidizes court programs and other court operatives while also growing a corporate structure that maximizes profits for the family court system. Thus, we claim that family courts are engaging in racketeering.

The stripping of the protective parent

In this assembly-line processing center, the protective parent is stripped of custody and then desperately seeks to have contact with the child, who is in the hands of the abuser. This makes the protective parent vulnerable to the blackmail and threats of the court, which assumes massive and overwhelming power over assets, property, and income by dictating the flow of funds through child support payments.

The court will exercise a stranglehold on the protective parent, as the child support enforcement agencies can immediately file to gain access to liquidate bank accounts and levy liens on property and whatever assets are available.

Noncompliance can even result in the stripping of one's driver's license, with notifications to law enforcement and the insurance company, not because of any criminal activity but because of civil issues related to payment of child support. This can be life-threatening to one who depends on driving for income and family care.

The division of child support enforcement is an entity with a life and authority independent of the court, which can and does exercise the power to incarcerate, file liens on bank accounts, against property, suspend driver's licenses, and report such suspensions to insurance companies that insure cars. Many child support enforcement programs, under whatever title or statute, have become elaborate and lucrative sources of funds for the state. Thus, the flow of funds through the court system becomes the driving force in custody decisions, rather than the protections and support that protective parents and their children should be able to expect.

The financial punishments imposed associated with the deprivation of custody rights include the loss of access to all marital assets and the imposition of cost payments for everything the new custodian required to ensure custody never reverts to the protective parent.

Victims of annihilation are expected to silently and passively accept and live with the consequences of decisions that remove children into the isolation of custody with a sexual predator, violent physical abuser, and sadistic adult who can use and abuse a child.

CHAPTER 17

The winner of the spoils relishes the thoughts surrounding the victory, which may include how many ways can I inflict pain and suffering on those around me towards whom I nurse grievances and seek retribution.

In family courts child abuse is flourishing, along with the dismantling of families, removing helpless children from their beloved protectors, and yes indeed, countenancing the organized, conscious, willful trafficking of children.

Chapter 18

What We Are Seeing

Trauma and the effects of trauma—defining torture

The effects of trauma and concomitant behavior are not concepts with which many court actors have any familiarity, interest, or training. What they do know is "parental alienation." They do not know or care to know anything about trauma. Trauma complicates the court process; parental alienation simplifies it.

Those of us who do understand trauma are seeing evidence in the lives of children of very serious neglect, abuse, and even sadistic acts, while these acts are dismissed by the courts as untrue. Then the children are placed with abusers who use them for sex and "share" the child with others.

We are seeing parents who had years of no contact with children, even those who only recently learned of the existence of these children, who decided they wanted custody, perhaps to get child support, perhaps for darker reasons.

We are seeing children from one part of the country suddenly escorted onto a plane to be sent off to a parent that the child had not seen for years, if ever.

We are seeing documented cases of deplorable cruelty against children, with a protective parent who has fought for those children. We are seeing law enforcement, lawyers, and court actors who with depraved indifference have left these children to the most extraordinary misery, dooming them to life experiences that will leave deep scars.

Further, we are seeing judges, guardians ad litem, and so-called therapists suggesting that even if such acts occurred, the child must learn to "regulate their feelings." There appears to be no situation of abuse, no heinous crime, that allows for protection.

We are seeing the theme continue that children are wildly imaginative liars, with court orders being enforced to the horror or denial of onlookers and the desolation of the oppressed.

We are seeing children ripped from the bonds of true love and loyalty, having to survive in the clutch of trauma incest bonds. In the words and writing of one young teen who lived for years in terror, "I was once such a good kid and I am no longer."

We are seeing behaviors associated with practices of torture, including isolation, starvation, berating, sleep deprivation, forced physical contact/touching/rape, subliminal indoctrination through seemingly benign visual stimuli, and forced exposure to horror films. Also, in the case of children, we would include threats that if the child discloses what they have been subject to, or attempts to secretly make contact with the beloved parent, that parent will be sent to jail and the child will be responsible for that parent's incarceration, thus enforcing the internal, conscience, fear-driven demand of conscience with the external autocratic command expressed to dominate, overwhelm, and dictate actions against personal will and cooperation.

We are seeing some children becoming like their abusers and like their abusers passing on a legacy of predatory behavior. Those who identify with their mesmerizing psychopathic manipulators, or are rewarded for compliance with betrayal and amoral behavior, may become the lawyers, politicians, and judges who contribute to the erosion of a democratic society.

Children are warned not to report, or if reports are made, to say they lied or exaggerated the event, or they were forced by a parent to falsely report.

Deployment of techniques out of the books of MK Ultra military brainwashing, with the goal of monetizing children as commodities/chattel serves to transfer children into the hands of psychopathic parenting figures.

The suppression of evidence of family violence and fraud is accomplished via subliminal mind management where children are directed to reinterpret the abuse and exploitation experienced as something other, driving sanity to madness at the hands of some combination of clinicians and courts.

Traumatized children are left dazed. Their experiences evidenced by behavioral sequelae related to exposure to assault and abuse are argued to have occurred as a result of false accusations by a vindictive spouse. Children's accounts of abuse and suffering are credited as false reports stemming from an alignment with a hostile parent to impugn an innocent spouse. Spurious arguments confuse fact and fiction, victim and perpetrator.

We are seeing judges inflict further insults and injuries by having police forces at their disposal to carry out orders that harm victims, further forcing the child victims into the isolation of their abusers. A court that should have helped the children instead expresses willful malevolence toward those children. As a result, we are seeing generations of children whose lives are being irreparably altered by this malevolence.

Over the past 25 years, two generations of children who have interfaced with family courts have been subject to the abusive practices of judges who deny the existence of crimes against children, thus making it impossible to accurately report the number of suicides, "accidental" deaths, homicides, incidents of family violence that stem from the heartless rulings of cruel and sadistic judges and associated court actors.

The catastrophic impact on the children of ignorant, belligerent, court orders is massively destructive, destabilizing, and deconstructing all the work that has been done to grow healthy, happy, thriving children who heretofore were on a trajectory to become good people, good students, and good citizens.

The hubris of the court actors is evidenced in the autocratic directives that treat litigants as chess pieces on a board to be moved at the discretion of the judge with the implementation of the court factotum for results that leave children in survival mode, having to fend for themselves, being totally at a loss as to who to trust.

Court-induced pathology, confusion, interference with object constancy, and all elements of trust and loyalty are the products of trauma bonds created by the court-forced unification with an abuser. Forced placement of children with hated abusers can result in making the protective parent an object of hatred as well, because the child feels abandoned in the most dangerous of circumstances, finding themselves in a position to negotiate some sort of pathological relationship with the abuser for their survival.

Whatever the child might have become as to all things good, the malicious elements intruded by the psychopathic indifference of the malevolent court presence have altered that path most negatively on the incalculable many. The impact on the harmed individual, on all who love that person, the impact of empowering an abuser, and the message that sends to observers are not factored into court decisions that impact the society of the family community. The cost to society of the potential harm from a person because of who that person has become because of being injured, abused, and feeling entitled to abuse is incalculable. As of now, it remains invisible and not part of the public consciousness.

Sigmund Freud first posited the enduring analytic truth that "that which is not resolved is repeated" over and over again for the pursuit of the resolution of trauma and resurrection of damage experienced by the person, by the self.

From our files

An example of a "spoiled brat"
They think of the children as spoiled brats who need to learn a lesson.

One such "spoiled brat" came within hours of nearly causing her own death by starvation because she was beyond desperate to escape the ongoing sexual abuse by members of her household. She contacted the FCVFC in time for intervention to be arranged, so she was rushed to the hospital in a jurisdiction apart from her paternal custodial parent. Her life was saved by medical intervention and an Attorney General who took appropriate action, resulting in a very rapid custody transfer.

The trial court/family court judge took fourteen pages of a transcript to rail against the intervention of the FCVFC and levied massive financial retaliation against the mother for the mother's audacity to defy the directives that would have cost the child her life.

However, a custody transfer was issued by a criminal court as per criminal charges threatened against the father if he did not relinquish custody.

Children ignored in court

One account from our files tells of a child who walked with a distinct limp, diagnosed by a physician who understood and described exactly how the inflicted damage occurred. Her functioning, her physical appearance, and her demeanor were clear that suffering was occurring, yet no intervention took place and the word of the seemingly affable, colorful local preacher was accepted without a second thought. Later in many rounds of court hearings, the testimony of siblings and the protective parent, the abuse experienced by children and the spouse of the abuser was discredited by well-known hired guns. It took years to procure the freedom from suffering that never should have been sustained.

One five-year-old told of the man who masturbated beside her in bed each night, moaning and groaning. She said, "I can't get the sound of his voice and the noises out of my head." At *five years old* she had cut marks on her wrists and said she wanted to kill herself. A family court judge forced her into the "care" of this abuser.

A three-year-old exhibits behavior that gives every sign of her having experienced grooming for sexual activity. She is forced into the total custody of her abuser, and her protective mother is forced into seeing her at an occasional supervised visitation. The child pleads with her mother, "When can I come home?"

Quotes from judges from transcripts

Quotes from family court judges, taken from court transcripts across the land:

The parent is seriously, provably psychiatrically ill.

"What does that have to do with parenting?"

A father has been sentenced to prison for child rape, and placed on the sex offender registry.

"He has been in jail for ___ years, so he needs to be reunited with his children."

Children have made statements of lurid physical and sexual abuse, humiliating, and cruel behavior, in fear for their lives.

"You are a liar."

"I don't care if you say your father is forcing you to have sex with him and his pals. You are going to live with your father."

The abuser is often treated as a subject deserving sympathy. Poor guy. He is saddled with such ungrateful kids.

What a pornographer did
A mother sought to protect her young daughter from the polypharmacy drug addict, drug-dealing father who withheld food from his child until she engaged in perverted sex acts with him. He drugged her in her early years, filling her with terror of the mother from whom he stated he rescued her, stating that her mother abused her and then abandoned her.

This story was not true. When the mother finally wrestled the California courts to a police-escorted rescue, the child ran from her in terror, wearing multiple layers of clothes to hide her appearance as her current drug-hazed mind prevailed over the memories of her life with her loving mother and their early life together.

The father's endless cash flow was infused by a combination of his pornographic artistry and his drug dealing. The father, an artist, whose work was greatly in demand, largely for dealing with Betty Boop babies and creative, colorful pornography, allowed him to hire legal talent more than willing to defend and promote the Father's Rights fairy tale forged to defend his petition.

The pornographer's attorney brazenly bragged that she had defended more than 650 such cases and had prevailed in all of them. However, the Foundation for Child Victims of the Family Courts was able to hold her accountable to the bar association and see her separated from her law license.

When the pedophile parent realized he had lost his lawyer, he forwarded massive amounts of pornography to

FCVFC computers as well as hundreds of subscriptions to pornographic magazines and snuff films from the dark web. The private phone lines and cell phone lines of staff were disseminated to johns ordering prostitutes, calling at all hours of the day and night, in multiple languages, from multiple locations.

The FBI removed the material accumulated as evidence of greater additional crimes, but no relief was found in the family courts.

Custody transfer is destroying children

Court orders create the ticking time bombs for suicides of young children and teens and the slow, agonizing deaths by drug or alcohol addiction.

We have yet to tabulate the cost to society of those who become predatory monsters, emulating the monsters who compelled them, molded them, drilled into their helpless bodies and minds the noxious behaviors that would break their spirits, destroy their minds, their characters, and the promise of the people they might have been.

The mass murderers, rapists, and serial killers spawned by the new genre perhaps never before seen in history are now before us in the form of a judicial system, specific to dependency, juvenile and family courts.

Chapter 19

The Public Health Crisis

A sinkhole / black hole/ criminal enterprise

We refer to the psychopathic presence of the court because of extensive up-front, close, and personal encounters with an indescribable, irrational, and unconscionable level of purely sadistic cruelty on the part of innumerable judges and zero experience to the contrary that has been noted over fifteen-plus years of uninterrupted, intense practice. The literature is filled with accounts of brutal child murders, murder-suicides, and suicides of children who stated that they "could not take it anymore." The suffering of survivors who emerge from isolation in the hands of cruel and sadistic abusers, placed in such circumstances via the alignment and collusion of a judge who set the path for separation of children from a protective parent was always clear as to the deterioration of the child/children in the hands of the abuser.

Driven by greed and lust for power, manipulation of the loose legal standards of family courts—paired with judicial discretion—has created a black hole that has allowed, using the language of astrophysics, the "spaghettification" of the body: the gravitational force that compresses a body from top to bottom while stretching the body at the same time. The process that begins the fall into a black hole in the astrological universe is an event called "a slip over an event horizon, a point of no return." It is postulated that the subject locked into a black hole of this nature cannot escape or see out from the inside—and no one from the outside can see within.

Such is the plight of innocent litigant protective parents within the black hole and black heart of family court litigation in the age of parental alienation and theorist constructs that illegitimately justify whatever cruel and sadistic dictates those judges who issue illegal orders can get away with.

The cults and their killing fields

Over the past 25 years, the power of the family courts has become progressively more coercive, controlling, and destructive. Every piece of evidence indicates that they are engaged in the billion-dollar industry of child trafficking. The FCVFC has clear and convincing evidence of two judges named in articles discussing cases that describe massive violations and cruelty as well as transferring children into the custody of fathers who are known to be engaged with trafficking agents associated with a national and internationally known trafficking group known as the Barbershops.

Reports to the FBI on each of our cases are routinely filed. Intervention is desperately needed at the level of investigating judges and collusion among court actors that allow criminal collusion and multiple forms of child trafficking to overwhelm society. Intimate knowledge of child trafficking practices is on display as purveyors of criminal acts project the implementation of their crimes on others as they enact crimes, accuse innocents, and function openly in the public arena.

To facilitate their unholy mercantile mission, the courts have progressively adopted the language of religious cults, authorities, and pretenders to ex cathedra authority speaking for God.

Cult communities progressively limit the capacity of their followers by maintaining the vice-like grip of whatever autocratic orthodoxy is held up as an ultimate authority. They produce a lemming-like population, ready to go over a cliff rather than be abandoned by the herd.

Simple formulas, simple directions for a life lived under the autocratic control of limited instruction: "Follow the rules and regulations, with no rights to independent thought, action, or protection of one's children."

The persuasion syndrome of cults is not dissimilar from the life-destroying court orders of judges. Bad judges can implement worse rules in the course of punishment for any disobedience or any attempt to even reasonably respond to unreasonable demands of child transfer into the hands of abusers.

Family court orders punish and persecute, purely to reward the elite who reap the benefits of money, power, and sex, providing access to the vulnerable population for the perverted power of child abusers within the confines of an intimidated and silenced population.

Protective parent "rebellion" is met with coercive control, court orders that are implemented by thug transporters, removing children from good parents into the punishing authority of reunification programs such as Family Bridges, as well as others, with providers across the country who operate under the same authoritarian seal.

Anyone who has suffered in another country through the indignities of being subject to the corrupt alternate upside-down universe of mind control, forced adjustment to watching your children's and your own lives destroyed in front of you, would not have been able to imagine that such repressive, wrongful autocratic impositions could exist within the democratic society of the United States of America.

Family courts have become arenas where there is little to no law, where ignorant, presumptuous, self-serving judges can override hard evidence and expert witness testimony.

The U.S. kangaroo family courts across the country have become killing fields. In courts that are wholesale transferring children into the hands of their abusers, we have an atmosphere of working in the world of child genocide. Those who have crimes to hide and assets to forge push through a legal and social campaign that smothers the atmosphere, extinguishing oxygen to breathe truth into the unfolding events of life with an abuser, and destroying any attempts to fight back.

But well-socialized, law-abiding, rational people have such faith in the U.S. justice system that warning them about family court often tends to be a useless proposition. They do not have a paradigm for the corruption and the depravity that define every step of the family court process.

But it's fine

On the list of behaviors for our children and youths, in the family courts, it seems that

- Incest—is fine.
- Spreading sexually transmitted disease—is fine.
- Having multiple sex partners, male and female—is fine.
- Paying prostitutes for sex, whether married or single—is fine.
- Forcing your children, however young, to have sex with their father—is fine.
- Forcing your children to have sex with their mother—is fine.
- Teaching young children to engage in sexual practices and acts with each other—is fine.
- Forcing young children to engage in sex with those who their parents care to share them with whether for free or pay—is fine.
- Teaching/forcing children into engaging in sexual acts while posing for photography, alone or with each other—is fine.
- Making sure children are forced to adhere to the "new standard"—which allows all these things they find to be abhorrent, painful, fearful, causing them to become dysfunctional, overcome, tormented—not only is this fine but it is demanded, insisted upon under penalty of torture.

It is a public health crisis

Family court judges exercise unconscionable use of force, manipulation, and control, insisting that children who have clearly, visibly been beaten, have broken bones and torn vaginas and bruised penises, be thrust into the hands of those who have abused them.

Children are called liars, and the protective parent is called an "alienator." Judges use court orders for "contempt" to separate little ones as young as two and three years old from parents trying to protect children from their abusers.

Family courts have turned into forums reminiscent of the Torchinadas Courts of the Spanish Inquisition. "Truth" is now declared against all evidence, and terminology is twisted. The child is separated from the protective parent and isolated with the "devalued" or "alienated" parent, or as we know them, the parent who has viciously abused a child.

These litigations are conducted through violations of due process, abuse of process, witness intimidation, suppression of evidence, failure to allow children to speak, excessive use of proxy interpreters of evidence (psychological evaluators, therapists, reunification therapists, supervised visitation therapists), and wide-ranging judicial discretion to insert evidence and facts that are not only not present in the court proceedings but can be factually proven to have never taken place.

These broken children often even lose faith in the parents who loved and fought for them as best as they could. They have become the trophies of sadists who force them into surrender and then interpret surrender, hopelessness, and helplessness as success.

CHAPTER 19

In the face of overwhelming odds stacked against them through the affiliation of professionals who pervert their scholarly treatises into psychobabble garbage, these children are taught to deny their thoughts, feelings, and experiences. They learn that opportunism, materialism, narcissism, and sociopathy are rewarded.

A poison is running through the veins of our courts, metastasizing through the country and gaining strength. This poison enriches those who peddle false narratives and reward sociopaths. This poison is destroying generations of children. We are facing an immense public health crisis in the name of "justice."

Chapter 20

It's Time to Believe the Children

There is not now nor has there ever been a golden age for children.

There are no civil rights for children, no laws to protect them, and no authorities, even parents, allowed to authentically, and authoritatively speak for children, as children have no rights.

Children have always been the first indentured servants. Childr en were used as workers in the mines, fields, and factories. Children were slaves before there were slaves because their parents enslaved them. Children were the first and most easily accessible sex objects (other than animals, and even animals gained rights to protection before children were recognized as subjects worthy of and requiring legal protections).

Children are not loved by many in our society and are not protected by our courts. Children are propagated, their bodies cultivated by breeders for breeding. The breeding agenda is then driven by those who control the currency and the currency controls the narrative, the imagination, and then the power to motivate the masses. Once a death grip is secured, the body (politic) is overpowered.

Laws and statutes can be stolen and bought with dark money in back rooms. Or no longer even in back rooms but rather in the vestibules of courts, where criminals openly ask, "How much for your testimony." Over many years the FCVFC has experienced this disease of the family courts.

Childhood, for many, is the road traveled from the lust and carnal knowledge that conceived them to the sickness of the minds of criminals that cause them to be exploited in the pornography field, where adult "members" (body parts) are pushed and shoved into baby parts at a time when the testimony of victims cannot be secured. The small victims cannot describe who did what to them, when, or where. Questions such as "Were the perpetrators tall or short, fat or thin, black, white or other. What time of day or night, where was your mother, did your mother tell you to say these things," and so forth.

When children are too young to speak, this makes them perfect victims, both for the sick perpetrator of crimes and for those ignorant of developmental stages and that there are more than the limited, hackneyed forms of questions to gather evidence and prove that crimes have been committed posed by the supercilious "gotcha" crowd.

In today's world of equal opportunity abuse by old and young, men and women, any ethnic or economic group, crimes committed against children, babies to late teens, any household beset with the misfortune of having to appear in a United States juvenile, dependency, or family court may expect that the criminal will be exonerated of whatever beastly crime he or she cares to indulge.

To the abuser goes the spoiled, desecrated children, to indulge appetites of the depraved, to silence complaints and protests, to destroy the person, the promise of who they might have been, to destroy core relationships of primal importance as the source and vehicles for nurturing trust, independence, the freedom to think, explore, be curious, be brave, be confident.

If you are a father, mother, or sibling with appetites from the crude to the most depraved you will find refuge in the kangaroo courts populated over years of testing the boundaries of depravity set loose through the writings of Richard Gardner MD. Gardner, whose private population of men accused of engaging in incestuous behavior within the context of marriage dissolution, became the testing ground, the small "n" for the test population he created to support the theories he constructed to provide (fabricate) evidence for a theory that defended and proved to exonerate men accused of sexual abuse of their children.

"Reasonable doubt" based on what has evolved to the edited theories reduced to the buzzwords "alienation" and "coaching," accompanied by the infamous protocol of separating and isolating children from their beloved parent, these words have become as terrifying as the slogan "Work sets you free," appearing over the entrance to Auschwitz, propagating the disease throughout.

The theory that Gardner constructed and then elaborated upon—for purposes of injecting probable cause into testimony that would have once been considered ironclad proof of guilt—came from no place other than Gardner's imagination. Gardner's hateful view of women as expressed throughout his writings, his never-vetted, never-tested theories that described women as spiteful and vindictive, in need of removal from the household if they interfered with the male prerogative—all these grew to become the prevailing method for dealing with all custody dispute, all custody litigation. The cottage industry that snowballed as a result took over discretionary law and hired-gun expert witness testimony, not driven by science or expertise, but by the laws of street mobs.

The ravaged bodies of babies, toddlers, and children trafficked through the pimps and madams of family courts, their bodies chattel, comestible and consumable, ravaged, reused, ravaged, ignored and disposed of, has become the law of the land as ignorance, arrogance, and concealed court rule has advanced from the 1980s to the present.

Hostility toward vulnerable, dependent subjects is in the DNA of survival of the fittest. This is the sickness of the family courts.

In today's world, the controller of the narrative, the message that grips the imagination and motivates unfiltered rage, not blocked or even slowed by education, knowledge, or science that drives impulsive action, this narrative intimidates, terrifies and overwhelms the controls that put the brakes on impulsivity. The thoughts that inform any public sense of decency, civility, and goodwill never have a moment to take hold as they are trampled, and pulverized into oblivion.

The racists represented by and through the original doctrines envisioned by Adolf Hitler's right-hand man Heinrich Himmler and subsequent racist ideological protagonists who orchestrate prejudice and force ignorance, such as Richard Gardner, represent agendas directed by ambition and greed.

Authoritarian, autocratic ideologies cause self-aggrandizing "leaders" to exalt themselves as superior powers. But this is not the only way this sickness manifests. In the family courts, lusters after power content themselves with identification with whatever bully seems prepared to protect, appoint and reward followers for sycophantic adulation and grunt work. Why work hard when you have money to pay others to cripple a populace through the family structure and through undermining the potential of children?

Yes, their vision appears to be to rule an injured, crippled populace, crippled by the injection of children whose minds and bodies have been destroyed by the abuse and the denial of the existence of abuse in all forms.

What we are witnessing via the forced denial of adult abuse of children, adult-on-adult abuse through domestic violence to which children are subject, is induced societal insanity driven by witness intimidation and mass terror.

If the role of the dependency, juvenile and family courts once geared to support, regulate implement, and teach citizens to function in a democratic society has become redesigned to in fact tear down the fabric of protecting the family system, the democratic ideals once espoused, then terrorizing adults and torturing children into shadows of whom they might have been most certainly an effective vehicle for undermining a democratic society in a most sinister manner.

It is a lie to tell children that parents are part of you so you must come to terms with even a "bad" parent. We would like to point out that a cancerous tumor is "part of you" as well. But when that tumor attaches itself to a body part or an organ, the tumor must be cut out for the body to survive.

The cells of that tumor do not need to be embraced or given the run of your body. No, they need to be treated, such as with radiation and chemotherapy, so that the infected cells may be hunted down and removed.

However, carrying their own sickness, courts across the U.S. function with horrifying unanimity of language and design, committed only to bellowing the Big Lie that any abuse claimed does not exist, never existed, and is purely a fabrication of some false claim, some spiteful vendetta by the accuser. The toxic application of reunification therapy is then compelled by the courts as criminals conspire for mind control.

Do Not Believe Them. This is the same way cancer spreads through the body, to cripple it and kill it. Instead, it must be eradicated.

PART FIVE

Onward and Forward

Chapter 21

The Story Behind the Defamation Case I Lost

In 2008 a Connecticut woman was divorced from an alleged abuser. She and her ex-husband shared joint custody of their two daughters, ages 5 and 8 at the time of the divorce. Over time, though, the children expressed increasing distress about their father, expressing desires not to be left alone with him or even to see him. Attempts at establishing any boundaries or controls failed, even as the children became increasingly verbal as to their specific complaints about their father. Their older half-sister, in graduate school, played a significant role as their protector and the person who filed complaints with DCF about the father's abuse of the children.

Raising the issues that had been brewing for years meant going to family court, which proved disastrous. In family court, the father teamed up with custody evaluator Eric Frazer Ph.D. Frazer was retained and paid exclusively by the father.[75]

---

75 See "Defendant's Post-Trial Brief," Scott Powell, Plaintiff v Jill Jones-Soderman, Defendant, posted at https://fcvfc.org/wp-content/uploads/2020/12/Defendants-Post-Trial-Brief.pdf

The false allegation created by Eric Frazer stated that this mother, a well-respected medical professional, was afflicted with Munchausen by Proxy, a diagnosis so toxic that the court moved to remove the children as soon as the words of this incorrect diagnosis wafted through the air. The mother was adjudicated as too dangerous to be near the children. Every effort she made to de-escalate tensions was used against her and the children, as this hostile evaluator attacked and mocked them. They were called liars; they were insulted and denigrated to their faces.

This evaluator's report would never have sustained a credible review. His fictional evaluations were incompetent to a professional eye, but they were embraced for their ability to be weaponized by lawyers litigating under the fake rubric of "parental alienation."

Furthermore, the judge in this case suppressed the children's testimony: they were not allowed to speak, to cry out for rescue from their alleged abuser. The father, along with evaluator Frazer, prevailed. So, at the ages of 8 and 11, these girls were removed from their mother, being told they were not allowed to see her because she was crazy and dangerous. The court granted the father authority over whom the girls could see or communicate with.

When their beloved and protective older half-sister suddenly died in 2014, they were devastated. But in their father's home, they were not allowed to speak of the sister they loved but he despised.

The girls were allowed supervised visits with their grandparents for 30 minutes per grandparent, on major holidays, Thanksgiving, and Christmas. They had to see each grandparent separately, meeting at a diner. The court order decreed that the girls could see these grandparents at any other time the father directed. But for him, this meant never.

The children were allowed brief visits with their mother under the supervision of a paid individual who monitored and edited interactions. These visits were reduced to something akin to small talk between strangers, depressed by the strain of wanting to break loose to cry and seek comfort in their mother's arms. Instead, they functioned like robots, internalizing their rage and grievances ... until they decided they had enough.

The girls' agony was expressed in symptoms of acute anxiety and depression. They had been medicated, hospitalized, and placed in special school programs for emotionally disturbed children. One child was seen by a psychiatrist (whom she doubted spoke English) once a month for 10 minutes, the time it took to renew prescriptions.

Their "therapy" consisted of having to meet with "therapists" chosen and supervised by Eric Frazer, the fraud who destroyed their lives. Their father sat outside the door as they met with the so-called therapist who then met with their father to "discuss their progress."

The girls were repeatedly informed that if they "told on their father" and disclosed the abuse they were suffering, they would be sent to separate foster homes, outside of Connecticut, and they would never see each other or any members of their family again.

Brilliant children were confined to substandard educations, languishing with truly psychiatrically disturbed children in a psychiatric-day-hospital-like atmosphere. But court operatives described the children as going to school and doing well.

When the FCVFC got involved

In July 2015, the distraught but persevering mother found the Foundation for Child Victims of the Family Courts through an internet search and reached out to me. She told me about the abuse she and her two daughters claimed to have experienced at the hands of her husband. I began reviewing thousands of pages of documentation.

The first step I wanted to take was to report Eric Frazer to the psychology licensing board. But to do that we needed to have certain records on the girls, and as things stood that release had to come through the father, who had full custody. So that avenue was blocked. Had we been able to file a suit for malpractice against Frazer, we could have filed for discovery and subpoenaed all documents. We could have called witnesses who would have detailed their observations of any criminal actions against the children and their mother. But at that time there was nothing we could do about Frazer.

So we took a different tack, pursuing the truth over the following months.

The FCVFC's immediate work with the children's mother was to clear her name of the heinous defamatory statements that accompany the Munchausen by Proxy diagnosis. This diagnosis never in any way applied to her.

Accordingly, we engaged one of the reigning experts of the time, Eric Mart, Ph.D. Dr. Mart was an expert in the diagnosis and treatment of those referred by courts for his evaluation and reports. We had worked with Eric Mart in another case in which the mother, an MD, was accused of being a danger to her children because of the Munchausen by Proxy diagnosis.

We also had the mother undergo neuropsychological testing, to rule out any subcategories of diagnoses that could be a co-syndrome of Munchausen disorder. Our client was well and fully documented as displaying no symptoms of this disorder. Her issues were consistent with the trauma of losing children in litigation to an abuser and having been maligned and blamed in court for wrongdoings of which she was not guilty.

Through these two medical evaluations, our client was completely cleared. First, she did not qualify as a Munchausen by Proxy diagnostic candidate. Second, she did not exhibit symptoms related to any form of psychopathy or disqualifying personality disorder.

To challenge the Eric Frazer fraudulent evaluation, we retained attorney Alex Schwartz of Connecticut. A clear understanding was written and a retainer was agreed upon, to confront the smear campaign presented by Eric Frazer's fraudulent psychological evaluation. The plan was to seek custody reconsideration so that the children could go back to the custody of their mother.

We were also putting in place plans to subsequently sue Eric Frazer for malpractice.

However, attorney Alex Schwartz never took the simple steps that would have cleared the targeted parent. He never filed a simple motion for reconsideration based on new evidence. Alex Schwartz never even called or contacted these professionals, nor did he return their calls when they tried to contact him. As a result, the mother was not cleared of the heinous allegations against her, and when the children did escape, she was not able to see them, as she would have been in contempt of court.

We did everything to give Alex Schwartz the tools for a successful, meaningful resolution of the case based on new evidence. But he did nothing to assist his client. As it became clear that he was not going to do his part to help clear his client's name and help her regain custody of the girls, we planned to file malpractice actions against him based on the violation of his retainer agreement.

However, a sudden new event aborted that plan.

The sisters contacted me for help

The very sudden new circumstances involved the arrival of two letters to the FCVFC from the children of my client, children from whom she had been separated for more than five years by that time.

By this time, having studied and worked on their case for about eight months from the perspective of their mother and the 2011 court proceedings, I was intimately familiar with many circumstances of their lives and all court proceedings, except for the parts that were sealed in juvenile court. I had reviewed thousands of pages of transcripts and filings, conducted interviews with their mother and grandparents, and engaged in personal communications.

But these girls discovered the Foundation through their own online search. Much later I learned some of the reasons the girls reached out to me: they had become aware of our position on Eric Frazer and our assistance to other children in the community that these girls knew.

Wednesday, March 20, 2016

To Whom It May Concern (FCVFC),

My name is [redacted]. I am 15 years old. My younger sister and I need your help. I have researched your work and found you online. This coming weekend,

CHAPTER 21

my sister and I have plans to call a family friend to rescue us from the abuse of our father. You and I cannot meet, talk, or e-mail currently, but [my sister] and I will be making a film tape to send to you in case. We cannot take it anymore. I am praying for the best. Please do all you can. I will be in touch as soon as possible.

Thank you.
Yours Truly,
[Older sister]

The younger sister also wrote a letter, in which she stated that her father "has touched parts of our bodies that make us feel uncomfortable, physically hurt and threatened us, and really frightened me... It's really scary for me to tell people about the abuse because I'm scared that my dad might kill me."

The handwritten letters were accompanied by a video in which the girls stated that they had been abused for the five years they had lived with their dad. They told me they had made a pact, intending to commit suicide together if they couldn't out of their abusive circumstances within a very short time.

The next day the two sisters called me on the phone and spoke with me for about three hours, during which time they described the abuse they were experiencing. For example, the younger sister told me that just a few days earlier her dad had forced his way into the bathroom while she was completely undressed and stared at her, "smiling, laughing, sneering." The older sister told me that her dad had raped her twice when she was younger. They went on to relay accounts of physical, emotional, and sexual abuse, humiliation, pulverizing control, and denigration on an intimate personal level.

After I spoke with them, there was no question in my mind as to the sincerity of their message, which indicated to me as a clinician and a mandated reporter that these girls were absolutely serious and at imminent risk. I believed them.

One particular DCF caseworker, the subject of my numerous direct complaints to every level of DCF, addressed the child who had been cutting herself severely for years: "You are a lying cutter."

If the children's mother had reached out in any manner to assist them, speak with them, or attempt to rescue them, she would have been found in contempt of court. Given the venomously hostile environment that surrounded her, she knew that if she were to be found in contempt of court, she would be sent to jail.

I was on my own to figure out resources to help the girls escape.

The escape mission was accomplished with the help of grandparents in their mid-80s, whom the girls hadn't seen in over five years, and then with the assistance of the local police. The girls met and spoke with police briefly before appearing in court on Monday morning to secure a temporary protective order against their father, taking refuge with their grandparents as their only guardians.

When their father sued the police for keeping the girls from him the night they escaped, the police testified in their depositions that they had no question that the girls appeared terrified, were telling the truth, and needed to get to court on Monday morning.

That weekend, in order to secure the temporary protective order in court on Monday, the girls dictated to me their detailed complaints relaying information about life with their father. I helped them prepare their complaints for attorney Alex Schwartz and forward them to him. He did have in his possession the detailed descriptions of the girl's complaints

Attorney Alex Schwartz then made an appearance. He spoke with the girls by phone and met with them in his office Monday morning with their grandfather, just before the Protective Order hearing. During the meeting the sisters personally committed to these statements detailing the degrading, despicable acts to which they had been subjected by their father.

Alex Schwartz wrote up the temporary protective order form with the girl's statement. Then without my knowledge or anyone's consent, instead of having the two girls sign the complaint, he had the children's grandfather sign the form as if the complaints had been reported by him. The children's grandfather, a graduate of the Annapolis Naval Academy, was in his mid-80s. Because of an injury related to his service as a naval officer, he was extremely hard of hearing. Attorney Alex Schwartz set up the grandfather, having him sign a document under oath when he did not understand the implications of his signing.

Monday morning arrived, and at the emergency hearing Judge Erica Tindill granted the temporary protective order, referring to the father's alleged crimes as "heinous." The girls' hopes rose. Together in the custody of their grandparents, the two girls made it clear that they were willing to testify in court, before their father or anyone else. They made plans to testify at a court hearing the following month. When they arrived in court for that hearing, they rightfully expected to have access to a court that would listen to them and finally free them from their accused abuser who had sequestered them for years.

But as it turned out, things went very differently in the court than they or anyone who cared about them expected. These adolescents were prevented from giving testimony in their own defense. In addition, they were repeatedly charged with being liars.

Judge Erica Tindill also refused to confirm the written charges they had articulated in the protective order. Claims brought by the maternal grandparents were also precluded from being filed. Instead, Judge Tindill again asserted the silencing of crimes. The girl's allegations of abuse were declared to be unfounded.

The Tindill court blocked all filings. Judge Tindill stated that no party in the case could ever seek assistance for the children. Everyone—the mother, the maternal grandparents, mandated reporters—all were precluded from ever filing any action against the father. Any attempt to file any claim had to be returned to the Tindill court.

Not only did Tindill refuse to have the girls testify in court, which would have allowed them to make a true and accurate record for the first time. But also, she imposed her own version of events, twisting and distorting facts, leaving out critical elements about their lives and functioning. She found fault with not reporting to DCF, referring and deferring to Eric Frazer, and exhibiting incredible ignorance of how abused children and DV victims function.

The grandfather, whose name was signed to the temporary protective order form, was found to be in contempt of court. Tindill inserted herself on the record as an expert, commenting and drawing conclusions for which she was entirely unqualified. She made up "facts" that did not exist, such as her statement that she was sure that the grandparents were in fact in contact with their grandchildren during the five years of isolation. But the grandparents were never in contact with the children during any unauthorized meeting over the period prior to assisting in the girl's escape. After making up these thin-air "facts," Tindill drew conclusions from them and then ruled according to her novel, inaccurate conclusions.

The therapists told the children that if they disclosed anything, they would be sent to CPS foster care in separate states.

The Board of Health was rendered helpless as medical records for the girls were not able to be procured because their father as the primary custodian would have to sign to release any of their medical records.

When the children were turned back to their father's custody, Judge Tindill ordered cameras to be placed in the house. Except not in the bedrooms or bathrooms, the very places where his alleged crimes were perpetrated.

The court erased all claims of abuse, based on the false testimony of the same evaluator whose reports had facilitated the children being placed in jeopardy at ages 8 and 11. This evaluator, who the adolescents claimed had insulted and humiliated them, ultimately prevailed.

After this court decision, the children were repeatedly kept from any communication with those who had tried to help them. They continued to see the so-called therapists and so-called psychological evaluators, all paid by the father whom they had accused in great detail.

Because the voices of the children and any witnesses for them had been silenced in court, it became evident that the complaint in the public arena was the only way to speak out, to have any impact. That is, to publish an article on the FCVFC website. The facts were there and must not be denied. I was their voice: they planned, and I facilitated.

At every developmental stage of their lives, these children experienced physical and emotional neglect and abuse. It seems clear that the only way the girls could have been redeemed as truth-tellers would have been for them to have killed themselves and left clear and convincing evidence of the crimes, they accused their father. But perhaps even then, they would not have been believed.

The last letter

May 25, 2017

To Whom It May Concern

My name is [redacted]. I am 16 years old as of 17 April 2017. We have been in the custody of our father, [redacted], in New Canaan, CT. We were taken from the caring home of my mother when [my sister] and I were 11 and 8 years old. For years we have tried to seek help for the abuse we have been experiencing at the hands of our father. From multiple sources (social workers, therapists, doctors, etc.) we have been shut down, dismissed, and simply ignored.

CHAPTER 21

A man named Eric Fraser saw us back in 2011. He spoke with me for nearly 10 minutes. In that time, my sister and I tried to tell Dr. Fraser about the physical, emotional, and sexual abuse and what it was like for us when with our father. He did not listen and custody was given to him. Since then, we have made many complaints/explanations, only to be dismissed. Living here is a nightmare, and when things at home began to escalate and we feared for out safety, [my sister] and I tried to seek help.

In March 2016, my sister and I tried to call a family friend. When she was unable to help us, we decided to call our grandparents ... from a friend's house. Once we told our grandparents, who we haven't had contact with for years, about the lives we lived with our father, that we could no longer take, we went to the New Canaan Police Department.

When we were there the interview was cut short when the police told us "That's enough."

For roughly a month we lived in the care of our grandparents. It was the first time in years that I had hope. [My grandmother] tells me how happy she was to see our family once again after being apart for so long. We both felt safe and at home finally. However, we were sent back to our father's. I remember that day very well. I was shaking and I couldn't breathe. My sister called me on the phone yelling/crying. I didn't want to return to the living hell we had been in for years and finally escaped from.

We went to Norwalk emergency room with our aunt because we both would have rather killed ourselves. We told doctors, nurses, sitters, caseworker, anyone who would listen to us. [My sister] and I were told our only other option was foster care. If we did not go home with our father, we were told that we would be separated from each other. This was truly our worst nightmare because we have been each other's only support throughout this abuse for many years.

We are afraid of him in spite of the camera in the family room, our lives are still controlled by fear. I feel I have lost nearly everything but [my sister] and a bit of hope. We have been threatened, tortured, and intimidated recently, within the past week, our father canceled the closing interview with DCF/NCPD. We just want help. I have spoken out much about the abuse but have since been silenced and returned to our abuser. This is why I/we will not/cannot be asked to speak up again in front of him only to be, again, returned to the man who has destroyed our lives. I am near certain he will kill us. Please help. We are so afraid. We had no representation in court and nobody will listen to help us. We just want to go home.

Sincerely,
[Older sister]

Not long after the children were returned to their father, the older daughter left the household and was ultimately emancipated. The younger daughter remained in the father's custody.

The pattern of judges playing fast and loose with facts creates a record that they then rule upon—incorrectly—because they ignore the voices of the victims themselves and instead create their own fabricated "fact patterns." This is unacceptable on every level of jurisprudence.

Judges' support for each other's erroneous decisions, over time creating an entirely false narrative, undermines the entire credibility of the judiciary. It also destroys children's lives and the fabric of society.

On the record, the victims were silenced, discredited, humiliated, and abused again, by the authorities and court system who were appointed to serve and protect them. But court actors and proxy stand-ins must not be allowed to rob the children of their voices. Above all, we believe that the voices and statements of children must be heard.

The father's accusation of defamation

In early October of the same year, 2016, I received notice that I was being charged by the girls' father with defamation. The case went to trial in the fall of 2019. I lost the case and appealed it. I also lost the appeal, with the final decision being handed down in February 2021.

I assess that the judges in charge at every level of hearings thoroughly abrogated their authority and responsibility to protect children and all vulnerable populations. The hypocrites in black robes circled the wagons and protected their own. Instead of seeking the truth, the courts promoted the interests of judges and various court toadies who suppressed vital evidence at every stage of this trial process.

The defamation trial in the district court

In the defamation court hearing, the girls' father, who was bringing the lawsuit against me, quoted the precise statements lodged against him by his daughters in the protective order first granted by Judge Erica Tindill. While the district court judges exonerated the father, the record upholds the fact that he was guilty of every act of which he was accused by his two daughters.

Judge Robert M. Spector nodded smiling approval as testimony was read from the children's diary relating events of sexual abuse by their father as well as their feelings about what happened to them, stating the impact on each child. Once read, the diary was subsequently excluded from testimony.

What evidence was used to exonerate the perpetrator of harm against his children? It was the proxy reporters with their own agendas, whether it was to make money or preserve their relevance in the positions they held. Proxy speakers for victims, who can alter or indeed falsify the truth, should never be allowed to speak when it is possible to procure direct testimony from victims. Proxy speakers in the form of defective DCF caseworkers and hired gun "experts" prevent victims from speaking, reporting for themselves, and then being believed because what they are reporting is true, according to the analysis of law enforcement and trained psychological experts.

All evidence from the child victims was dismissed in favor of agencies and judges who betrayed their responsibility to the children. Judges and agencies I had criticized were held as authorities, as opposed to findings of abuse and neglect brought by an independent expert brought into the case by the victims themselves.

The agencies I had filed complaints against stated that I was negligent and malicious because I hadn't contacted them. But I had contacted them multiple times and then filed complaints against them because of their fraud, incompetence, and negligence. They made false statements that were contrary to the record. The FCVFC filed complaints against almost every individual and every agency in this case, because of extensive evidence of fraud and malfeasance.

When the case was appealed
On Thursday, February 4, 2021, a two-judge panel of the United States Court of Appeals for the Second Circuit heard oral arguments regarding the defamation case, in which the father of the two girls accused me of defamation. The questions and answers at the hearing covered the following territory:

1. *Did Jones Soderman believe the (allegedly defamatory) allegations against the girls' father that she made on her website?* That is stated in the district court record. She believed the children's allegations of abuse.
2. *Did she have* reason *to believe the allegations she wrote?* Yes, and abundant evidence was provided to the district court on this count, and to demonstrate the significant reasons she believed the children.
3. *But didn't she* purposely avoid the truth? No, she didn't. She believed the children.
4. *The fact that Ms. Jones Soderman* didn't report *these "outrageous and dangerous conditions," these "criminal allegations," means she didn't believe them. Why didn't she report them?* But she did report them, and also helped the children report. Evidence is in the documentation.
5. Malice *needs to be proven in the case of a public figure. Why are you claiming that malice needs to be proven in the case of a private individual?* Because this allegation [child abuse] is a matter of public concern.

6. *Are you saying you believe that there could be a* reversal *of the finding of the family court, which implied that these allegations of abuse are false?* Yes, if all evidence were to be allowed to be brought forward.

The Second Circuit Court judges reviewed the brief and responded to it by ignoring it and then creating "evidence" that was non-existent. They then supported a verdict of guilty regarding the defamation accusation. Details follow:

The fifteen minutes of the court hearing commenced with the attorney's statement that when speech is made in the public interest, the burden of proof to show both malice and falsity lies with the plaintiff (the father of the two girls).

The attorney stated that because Jill Jones Soderman believed the children's claims of abuse by their father, this belief precluded any finding of actual malice. The plaintiff failed to meet his burden of proof regarding both actual *malice* and *falsity*.

> *Judge response*: One judge argued that good faith (believing that what she said was true—that the girls' father was an abuser) would not preclude liability for defamation.

The attorney argued that case law shows that she must have "purposely avoided the truth," which she didn't, he argued. "Ms. Jones Soderman was acting in good faith because she did believe the children, and she had significant evidence supporting it."

> *Judge response*: Another judge asked, if your client is a mandatory reporter, why did she "not report these outrageous and dangerous conditions to the

CHAPTER 21

authorities? ... These are criminal things, criminal offenses."

Please note that the judge called the conditions in which the children said they were living "outrageous and dangerous." He said the claims they were making were of "criminal offenses." This judge had failed to note in the documentation that I had made multiple reports to several authorities, as described above.

The attorney argued that I had helped to facilitate the children's escape so that they could report to the police themselves.

Judge question: A judge asked, since the girls' father was not a public figure, why did a case of malice need to be proven? [The standard for defamation is higher for public figures than for private individuals.]

The attorney replied, "The case law... requires that in cases where the publication relates to a matter of public concern, then actual malice is a requirement and the plaintiff must bear the burden of proving actual malice."

This is the crux of the matter in this case. When we published about this case years ago on the FCVFC website, this was the only vehicle for exposing the truth. The judge had silenced every witness, including the two children who were abused. The public concern was that an alleged abuser was allowed to live free and without consequences in his community.

Judge question: "I want to ask a question about falsity... You make an argument that even if the finding [of Jones Soderman's statements being false] was made explicitly, that there was no evidence to support it."

So, if the previous court (the district court) had declared the plaintiff's (father's) testimony to be credible, the judge asked my attorney to explain how he could say that the record is insufficient to support such a finding.

The attorney responded at length. "When we consider only the evidence that is non-hearsay, admitted for its truth, there is very little [evidence to support the plaintiff's testimony as credible]. Essentially it boils down to the plaintiff's uncorroborated testimony and the 2016 Judge Tindill opinion." The attorney confirmed that if indeed the truth or falsity of my statements were to be examined, that finding could be reversed.

"*There is substantial evidence in the record contradicting [the plaintiff's] testimony that was admitted towards proof.* For example, the protective order, which was admitted for its truth in its entirety, details the children's allegations of abuse against him. There was also the children's conduct throughout the entire ordeal with Ms. Jones Soderman that suggest that they were telling the truth and that he was abusing them. After they found out that they were going to have to be returned—"

At this point, the attorney was interrupted for at least the second time.

> *Judge question*: "You say that the trial court found that Ms. Jones Soderman believed in the truth of her statements. And I'm just wondering if you could point us to where specifically she did that, where this is said."

CHAPTER 21

The attorney provided multiple examples from the district court statement. "*She believed the girls' allegations* in part because of their demeanor during their many phone calls and in the video they sent to Jones Soderman and because of the content of the letters and the detailed allegations in [their] diary entries." And again, "At the conclusion of the call, Jones Soderman believed that if she did not get them out of the house that weekend, they would go through with their pact to kill themselves." And again, "Jones Soderman conversely believed those allegations, with full knowledge of the case history and judicial orders."

As he was proceeding to give more examples, he was interrupted and told that the hearing was concluded.[76]

Now, by the ruling on February 4, 2021, the three judges of the Second Circuit Court of Appeals made it clear that children's rights mean nothing to them. Those who want to help the children who cry out to them with clear and convincing evidence that they are at grave risk, those helpers may be censored by court decisions.

Each point the judges made, and each question they asked, had a compelling answer with evidence to support it. None of the case law these judges brought to bear on this case pertained to the protection of children. Several times they cut off the attorney's responses in favor of their preconceived ideas.

It seems evident that these judges were uninformed and indifferent to the complex history and facts of this case, as well as the import of their decision to silence children who are being harmed.

---

76 The full hearing can be heard on the FCVFC website at https://fcvfc.org/wp-content/uploads/2021/02/Powell-vs-Jones-hearing.mp3.

And thus we stand. Correcting the courts, over and over again.

I want to make it clear that to this day I continue to be very pleased with the decisions I made in this case, most immediately because the children did not kill themselves and have moved on in their lives to have relationships with wonderful members of their family who had lived in fear and grief for years in their absence. I knew that the abuse they suffered at the hands of their arrogant, bullying father stopped as soon as I published, and no other action I could take would stop the abuse.

When speech in the public interest is censored

This was a crucial case of the First Amendment right of speech in the public arena. The decision could have helped to give a voice to children who seek rescue from years of abuse. Isolated children who were prepared to give testimony in court before their alleged abuser about the abuse they sustained were never allowed to give that testimony.

Children are silenced and pressed back into the isolation of their abuser because the false testimony of so-called experts can control a narrative that exonerates an abuser. Failure to properly address acts of incest and child abuse—is creating generations of home-bred criminals and adults whose lives are severely damaged.

Any system that promotes testimony filtered through proxy reporters, all of whom have financial investment and motives in providing a self-serving outcome, cannot possibly be relied upon to seek truth and justice, especially for vulnerable children. Embracing false narratives provides for the growth of cottage industries of professionals trained to lie, cheat, and steal and undermines the entire justice and court system of any nation.

The First Amendment must be unshackled, not only used to promote and protect wealthy criminals. Children—the victims themselves—must be seen, heard, and believed.

Chapter 22

Instead of Simply Cursing the Darkness, Our Clients Illuminate the Darkness

The FCVFC does not accept grants or donations with any strings attached. This is because we want to work for the benefit of protective parents in family court without having our allegiance drawn elsewhere.

Because of this commitment, we have been able to maintain unadulterated independence and the ability to focus solely on helping our clients. But this also means that we have never been the recipients of any meaningful amounts of private funding. Since our founding in 2007-2008, we have been supported entirely by our clients.

My work began with the naïve and probably self-protective view that if servants of the court simply understood the harm being experienced by children and families, that would be enough to induce reform.

It was with great disbelief and resistance to that disbelief that I was forced to abandon my rose-colored glasses and accept a very tough reality: that the perpetrators of harm that lived in fortresses girded by power and the authority of the law knew exactly what they were doing and were pursuing their own interests with a vengeance. That vengeance was directed at anyone who got in their way. Most people who got in their way were severely injured.

As I fought to not be removed, I was reminded that rethinking one's position is not a bad thing. Redefining one's position in life to tackle the goal has a much greater potential for success than simply being oppositional.

As a result, over the past many years, the Foundation for Child Victims of the Family Courts has been revealing, confronting, and reporting on the personality and character of judges who drive custody litigation that involves children being transferred from the custody of protective parents into the custody of parents who are credibly accused of all ranges of physical, sexual, and emotional abuse.

The Foundation has focused on the driving force of the Richard Gardner, MD, fabricated theory of parental alienation and denial of sexual abuse of children as a vehicle for creating reasonable doubt and eviscerating the ability of the protective parent to substantiate charges of abuse against the other parent in custody litigation. We identify existing laws and successful litigation that has prevailed in areas of concern to us, in order to follow precedent, building on the aspects of the work and developing the process to win cases.

Over the years, we have conducted in-depth background checks and research on the law associated with applicable local, state, and federal localities, as well as researching the criminal, personal, financial, and character analysis of each figure involved in the case, including judges, lawyers, court-appointed factotum, and other case actors.

We have sought to look for individual advantages as well as business, political, and family affiliations, seeking to trace the cash flow through the investigation and evaluation of tax documents and other types of financial documentation subject to analysis.

A great deal of our work and our writing has been focused on identifying individual judges, lawyers, psychological evaluators, and so-called therapists whose challenged characters have been described in terms of psychopathy and a willingness to engage in unconscionable criminal behavior. Accordingly, we have diligently sought the license removal of practitioners who have facilitated crimes against children and protective parents.

We use this information to in litigation to secure custody as well as to assist in the civil litigation against these crime facilitators and to seek prosecution of criminal acts of physical and sexual abuse.

Our fund of insight and understanding has increased greatly over the years, as have our skills at addressing core issues driving what amounts to child trafficking through family and criminal courts across the United States.

What makes our work successful

To maximize the help we offer, we have to have a very clear vision of our mission and how to accomplish it, as well as a clear picture of the population we serve.

Rather than simply standing in defiance of directives, we must define goals in a positive manner that will be effective in taking on the challenges ahead.

First and foremost, we have the desire to help and rescue and nurture a suffering population, the victims of the family courts: the protective parents, the child victims, the siblings, and extended family and friends. That began as the defining elements of the work that we set out to do.

With this in mind, the Foundation has continued to grow in the direction of expanding our vision to protect children and families from immediate harm, and even more, to understand the roots of that harm where these concepts came from in the first place, and to seek solutions.

We use the tool of evidence-based case evaluation as part of our plan to expose judicial fraud, corruption, malfeasance, abuse of power, and abuse of due process. Identifying and confronting these issues is a large part of what we do. We offer treatment strategies for mobilizing and supporting traumatized victims of vexatious litigation in family courts, to those who have been subject to deceit and financial ravages by various professionals who have made empty promises and left clients with nothing.

Knowledge of the practices in the court process is critical. *Facts* are the work product that we employ, not airy-fairy promises and wishes. We work to help clients understand their cases, the law on which their cases are built, and the remedies that we hope to deploy to effect positive outcomes.

We will continue to confront the lies and cowardly musings muttered behind our backs by those who seek to evade responsibility for their venal, corrupt action. We will confront them to their faces and in public litigation, supported by hard evidence with formidable experts who speak for and explain the cases of victims when they cannot speak for themselves.

Where crimes are suppressed, they must be exposed. Where there is "immunity," there must be accountability.

At the FCVFC not only do we seek to expose crimes against children, but we seek to have those criminals experience the moral and legal consequences of their actions. Financial recovery is a large part of those consequences, but one of our goals is for the voices and words of the child victims to be heard. These are the most compelling and consciousness-raising and conscience-searing experiences, not only for the remorseless criminals, but for anyone prepared to bear witness to those who have heretofore been silenced.

For the FCVFC, ending one form of intervention doesn't mean the end of the entire effort. It simply means beginning the next form of intervention. When a case is stalled, we go back to the beginning and rethink strategy. By doing this, we have developed new interventions directed at structural change. We hope that many will follow suit.

Children deserve to be able to live with the parent who will provide the most conducive environment for them to grow and thrive. Caring for, nurturing, and protecting children—these should be among our highest priorities as U.S. citizens. These values should be acknowledged as critical to the survival of a democratic society.

The FCVFC is determined to do everything we can to facilitate the protected childhood that children deserve and need.

We begin the process with an initial forensic evaluation of court records, testimony, and evidence, including the initial petition, motions, orders, and transcripts.

The focus of this forensic analysis is the review and evaluation of evidence that appears in a court case: evidence validity, flaws in evidence, evidence not provided, fraudulent evidence, evidence critique, evidence that needs to be provided to support the client's case, and so forth.

You will provide us with detailed personal histories, case timelines, information on witnesses, and other collateral contacts.

We will then formulate an intervention plan, review the recommendation with you, and prepare to move forward.

Based on an initial assessment, with a contribution by a variety of experts, we formulate an intervention plan and review our recommendations with you.

We will seek, if possible, to connect with an ethical attorney in your state. This is an attorney who wants the court to hear evidence and protect children more than wanting to line their own pockets. If we find one, he or she will then partner with one of the attorneys working with the FCVFC, in order to form legal strategies.

If a review of court transcripts shows that the judge is prejudiced in the courtroom, we will file a motion of recusal for that judge and petition for a new judge.

Forensic advocacy incorporates the continued analysis of complex material, as well as integrating such material into the litigation rhetoric. Capturing and translating our client's in-depth understanding of their case with our understanding of court dynamics creates a complete, thorough case litigation narrative.

FCVFC advocacy also extends beyond supporting the client in the immediate courtroom process. We also advocate in settings such as social services, doctors, and mental health professionals, and government and private agencies, such as public and private schools.

The Foundation goes beyond normally expected forensic and legal services, as we deal on a regular basis with both child abuse and "parental alienation." identifying factual information entwined with mental health and psycho-dynamic material always requires careful ethical expert witness testimony and a nuanced understanding of the multiple issues in play. This is what the Foundation strives to do.

Courts tend to deal with therapeutic intervention as an arm of the court process, often to "correct the thinking" of protective parents and children whose complaints of abuse and heinous crimes were considered by the court to be unfounded. The Foundation does not support adherence to this form of surrender to wrongful judicial orders.

What we do differently

A protective parent can lose the child custody battle in the family courts only by giving up or by continuing to follow the same unsuccessful procedure over and over. But there are many ways to win. In this nation of laws and free speech, there are little-utilized modes of intervention that need to be undertaken far more aggressively.

1. *We refuse to fight an accusation of "parental alienation"; instead, we fight this fraudulent concept*

    It has been made very clear in this case perpetrators will pay lawyers and the relevant group of associated fixers to accomplish their goal: to obliterate their adversary, the protective parent, with claims of "parental alienation," and to seize the children.

    As you know by now, the parental alienation argument is a ruse used to turn a child over to an abuser. Trying to defend the protective parent against this scientifically debunked, utterly corrupt theory only serves to give credibility to the debunked theory, causing the protective parent to have to be on the defensive.

At the FCVFC, we flip the PA protocol. Instead of trying to defend a client against it, we refuse to give it any credence at all. Instead of battling against the accusation, we battle against the concept itself.

2. *We file complaints against court colluders, and more*

When evidence of collusion and foul play becomes evident, any lawyers, experts, therapists, and all participants in the game-plan protocol of "parental alienation" must be reported to their licensing boards.

A "complaint" is a request for formal action, with judicial boards, bar associations, and other professional organizations that should hold corrupt court actors accountable. Writing a general complaint about a provider is inadequate. That complaint must be sent to the licensing board that supports this provider's services to the courts and the client litigant.

The Foundation for the Child Victims of the Family Courts is committed to filing complaints against court officials, expert witness providers to the courts, and all court actors who violate their fiduciary responsibility to their clients. We then publish those complaints on our website, as part of our writing that elucidates the core issues of concern to the Foundation and that benefit the client.

3. *We bring lawsuits for defamation and other crimes*

If we find that those accountable organizations are unresponsive, perhaps because of corruption, or if we find that criminal activity has occurred, we may begin lawsuit proceedings. Civil and criminal charges need to be brought against those who commit crimes against children—even those in the family court system.

Prosecution means pursuing removal of licenses for malpractice, the pursuit of financial damages, review of criminal activity, and referral for criminal prosecution.

Defamation lawsuits need to be brought against those who have defamed the protective parent. Claims of defamation must be prosecuted against the perpetrator who is seeking to destroy every aspect of the protective parents' life—reputation, income, friends, family—and leave the protective parent heartbroken, traumatized, and penniless.

4. *We deal with institutions, agencies, and medical professionals*

Neither the courts nor government entities take kindly to whistleblowers who jeopardize enormous sources of funding and financial opportunities. Government agencies, with their endless resources, viciously pursue those who speak on the part of vulnerable populations, especially vulnerable populations that are battling against formidable entities.

However, the Foundation fearlessly exposes cases of corruption and fraud when the client's or their child's reputation is at stake.

Dealing with government/administrative agencies is a major focus of engagement, strategy, and study. The Foundation focuses not only on issues related to individual cases, but the analysis, critique, and intervention that applies to agency oversight and public policy as well.

We often write letters to other people-helping organizations in the local community, bringing them to an awareness of the court corruption and the truth of the matter so they can also understand and take any action necessary to protect the children.

The Foundation for Child Victims of the Family Courts thus uses aggressive legal action, expert witness testimony, investigation of the source of corruption, publication of the machinations of such acts, and a rallying cry to the community in order to shine the light on the malefactors in the family courts.

Who is our ideal client?

Some who contact us but decide not to engage us have given up, having been defeated at some point in the litigation process because of humiliation, guilt, fear, a sense of hopelessness, or lack of energy or funding. Some of these contacts remain in touch with us for years, and as we continue to hear their thoughts and feelings unfold, learn from them and write about their concerns.

In many cases, these parents' children have been seized by the courts and transferred to the children's abuser. These parents have either had their rights terminated by the courts or live with limited visitation orders. Coerced consent orders are sometimes filed, where lawyers or judges inform the parent that unless some contingency is completed, that parent will never see their child again.

We encourage these parents to light the darkness instead of cursing the darkness.

Towards those ends, we accept clients carefully, after evaluation, scrutiny, and an assurance that the client understands and wishes to participate in the mission of the Foundation to support the drive to litigate and prosecute on behalf of protective parents seeking civil rights and constitutional protections for themselves and their children.

Every case we take on must be a model of the law of litigation practice, of the deployment of experts, and a roadmap for teaching court strategy in the areas of litigation practice and demeanor of litigants in court, to teach argument engagement in the interpersonal practice of being a presence in the court process.

We view our work with clients as a collaboration and an ongoing work in process—based not on empty hope, but an understanding that the process takes time and hard work. It also takes education on how the legal process works in family court. This can be a rude awakening.

Within that first family, the family described in Chapter 1 of this book, we found the multiple dimensions and parameters that came to define the population for us to serve.

The FCVFC was and is a small group with limited funding. We do not deal with grants or other outside funding, because we want no outside forces putting a thumb on the scales.

So from the onset, we needed to understand who was the protective parent that we were conceptualizing as the protective parent that we wished to deal with. We further refined those designations by setting out to have a full understanding of our client. And who would be our best client?

Ideal clients will overcome their fear
Our clients are fighting for custody. They come to us experiencing the magnitude of corruption and false information in the court.

They have often experienced trauma from different phases of their life, affecting their ability to trust, form relationships, and move forward. But these elements are critical because they need to understand the legal and psychological issues raging within this environment.

We want to be able to work together, despite fear, to rescue children from dire circumstances.

Our clients must be able to manage their fear while confronting a system fraught with fraud, malfeasance, and cruelty, and driven by greed, power, and self-aggrandizement.

Ideal clients will cooperate in working with the FCVFC as director of the case

When a client thinks he or she knows better than the FCVFC experts, when that person thinks of us as subjects to manipulate, telling us what to do and how to do it, thinking we are here to act as their agents and follow instructions, that client is impossible for us to work with.

We have had clients tell us which documents we are allowed to read, how we are to understand and interpret those documents, whether we can speak to their children, and how we should respond. We cannot be limited as to the broad scope of the material we need, and we will not be educated by our clients on how the family courts operate.

Ideal clients will be mentally stable

When parents are psychiatrically disturbed, it may take us a while to see it. While these cases are rare, they are certainly problematic. Any case that is not won strengthens the corrupt institutions we are working against. It also leaves child victims unattended and unable to be rescued.

One mother who contacted me began with a complaint that her ex-husband was trafficking her daughter. This is a familiar complaint, and I took her seriously. But as time went on, I heard that the daughter was being trafficked by her swimming coaches and other professionals in her daughter's life. It seemed that almost everyone in her daughter's life was trafficking her.

The daughter was removed from the swim team, which she enjoyed, and she lost many of her friends.

For the most part, the mother came across as intelligent, well-spoken, and well-organized. She gained the attention of law enforcement and other officials who launched investigations into all these professionals. But the investigation revealed nothing, and eventually, the school authorities launched lawsuits against her for defamation.

The child denied that she was being abused by these people, but the mother still insisted on it. She wanted her daughter to be institutionalized and have psychiatric care because of the horrors she truly believed her daughter was enduring. Her psychiatric derangement was a danger to her daughter, who ended up separating herself from her mother.

We did try to work with the court to help them understand that the mother wasn't lying but truly did believe these psychotic allegations, and she needed psychiatric care. This kept her out of jail for what would otherwise have been seen as contempt charges. But our offers of assistance in this way were not what this mother wanted, so she filed complaints against the Foundation, making allegations consistent with her level of psychosis. They would have sounded reasonable to anyone unfamiliar with her case and situation.

This woman had gone through over 130 attorneys, each of whom eventually understood the situation and removed themselves from the case, except for one charitable group who continued to be kind to her, and to me as she launched complaints against me.

Here is an example of one of her emails to me:

Hey Dumbo Rapist:
I still have not received my $5000 back plus a quadrillion dollar in damages for every penetration and rape of [my daughter] who is still not home, you dumbo, worthless whore!

And yet she continued to work as a kindergarten teacher and was never discharged from employment.

Ideal clients will persevere when the work is long and difficult Some people think they want to protect their children and do what's right, but they're exhausted. They want a life for themselves and don't want to continue the fight with their ex-spouses. Perhaps they have a new life at their fingertips, and they want to move on.

That's the situation with parents who say they want to do the work and protect their children, but when it comes time for them to do work that needs to be done, they do not do it.

One mother failed to file a critical motion. As a result, her children were moved to the next phase of reunification with a dangerously aggressive and fear-inspiring predator, which resulted in severe damage to the youngest remaining children who were unable to be extracted from contact with the father.

Here is an edited and redacted copy of the termination letter I sent regarding that mother.

Please be advised that I am writing to you to advise you that [the mother], mother of [three children],

children at grave risk of harm, failed to take critical action to protect her children from custody transfer into the hands of the children's accused abuser.

[This mother] had been a client of the FCVFC as of [date]. [The mother's] engagement with the FCVFC was terminated as of [date].

As per our work discussions and agreement with you, it was the assessment of experts working with this family that it was critical for the welfare, and physical and emotional survival of these children that custody matters required careful management. Work with the Foundation for Child Victims of the Family Courts involved assessment and interventions on multiple levels discussed and agreed to with [this mother].

Most critical of immediate concerns was that custody of the minor children remain with [the mother]. That custody arrangement came under jeopardy as the father, documented abuser/danger to the minor children's psychiatric functioning, filed a motion for a transfer of custody of the three minor children.

The multi-level/multi-disciplinary interventions planned and approved by [the mother] were developed and implemented.

The motion responding to the children's father's motion to transfer custody was prepared by the legal division of the FCVFC for [the mother] as a pro se litigant. It is attached for your information, as proof of her discussion with the legal team and her agreement to electronically file the motion, which was acutely time sensitive. She was fully aware that if the response to Father's motion was not filed in a timely manner that the children were at risk for custody transfer.

> *Without notice to or prior discussion with any member of the FCVFC team involved in her case, [the mother] failed to file the legal motion prepared for her. We became aware that the motion was not filed when confirmation of filing was requested. As per the attached email indicating "No," the motion was not filed.*
>
> *After a brief, contentious, uninformative discussion with [the mother], all work with the Foundation for Child Victims of the Family Courts has been terminated based on serious breach of trust and [the mother's] immediate betrayal of her responsibility to the welfare of her children, as per the assessment of the experts dealing with this case.*
>
> *Jill Jones Soderman*
> *Executive Director, FCVFC*

A consciousness of the veil of grief, mourning, and profound sadness

We stand with parents who fight with everything they have to protect their children. We work with them to fight through a terrifying present to provide for a joyful future.

This population is the majority of the clients that we work with, but we are constantly mindful of and live with the thoughts of those lives, though not our clients, those lives lost by murder or suicide as well as those whose life force has been exsanguinated by being sold into the depravity of life in isolation with an abuser. On behalf of those children who we view as victims and martyrs, we seek to empower the voices of children who are or have been locked into the court-created hell where they are subject to the abuses of a predator parent and an equally predatory, autocratic court system. We want to help these children before they disappear into despair or become the abuser they could not escape to become the selves they might have been.

In the words of poetess Jaki Shelton Green, "I Want to Undie You."

> *I want you to un-die, come back*
> *I want the hush of you un-hushed*
> *I want the cries of you un-cried*
> *I want the grief of you-ungrieved*
> *I want the scream of you un-screamed*
> *I want to un-steal the stolen of you*
> *I want to un-confuse the confusion of you,*
> *Un-steal the stolen of you,*
> *un-murder the murdered of you,*
> *un-butcher the butchered of you,*
> *unwound the wounded of you*
> *unbound the bondage of you*
> *un-sterilize the sterility of you*
> *un-deny a life denied to you*
> *un-seal the sealed of you*
> *un-mask the masks of you*
> *un-veil the veils of you…*
> *un-sacrifice the sacrifice of you*
> *un-erase the erasure of you*
> *un-lock the locked of you*
> *un-take the taking of you*
> *un-still the stillness of you*[77]

---

[77] Jaki Shelton Green, *I Want to Undie You*

Rest in peace, Rashad, as your short life was made a living hell by monsters who will go neither unnamed nor forgotten. You are our North Star and the light that leads us as we work on behalf of the child martyrs who have lived dazed in darkness and confusion.

Those who illuminate the darkness

Clinical forensic experts are also a critical part of our team. These experts can present complete reports that lay out the issues and the claims as to who did what to whom and how this happened. The clinical forensic expert can discuss and describe the impact on the child and can make recommendations for care and custody to repair damages to the child and family. Unlike many court actors, they truly have the "best interest of the child" at heart.

We are now at a point of epiphany. We are partnering with those who are the best and brightest, with incredible character and brilliance. The Foundation praises the work of the many honest, ethical, hard-working individuals who work in the legal and judicial realm, whose work, efforts, and reputation are impaired by fraud and abuse of power. They, along with our clients, are the ones who illuminate the darkness.

A last word

In the case of exploration and confrontation in circumstances of acute criminality and tragedy, it is not enough to explore, describe, and explain events. The problems presented must not be left to remain in place in a passive and hopeless stance of resignation.

It is our position that one must resolve to meet the challenges of such tragedies with solutions for intervention and change. So in the spirit of hopefulness and expectation that all of life's tragedies can be the subject of learning, growth, and change, the Foundation for Child Victims of the Family Courts is embarking on developing an accountability program. This will begin with the initiation of instruments to gather as wide a swath as possible of information, to capture the experiences of litigants before the courts that break down the elements of who is doing what to whom and the outcomes experienced in a manner in which the specific court actors who enjoy immunity and escape accountability will become accountable as per the broadest possible capturing of the experiences of the public.

We look to learn from our own experiences, share the facts, and implement programs, to create a better future for others.

Bibliography

deYoung, Mary. "The World According to NAMBLA: Accounting for Deviance," The Journal of Sociology & Social Welfare, 1989, 16(1), Article 9.

——. "The indignant page: Techniques of neutralization in the publications of pedophile organizations," Child Abuse & Neglect, 12(4), 1988.

Gardner, Richard. Child Custody Litigation: A Guide for Parents and Mental Health Professionals, Creative Therapeutics, 1986.

——. "Clinical Evaluation of Alleged Child Sex Abuse in Custody Disputes," Innovations in Clinical Practice: A Source Book, Volume 7, edited by Peter A. Keller and Steven R. Heyman, 1988.

-——. -. The Parental Alienation Syndrome, Creative Therapeutics, 1998.

——. "Qualifications of Richard A. Gardner, M.D. for Providing Court Testimony," Richard A. Gardner. http://richardagardner.com/cvqual

——. Sex Abuse Hysteria: Salem Witch Trials Revisited, Creative Therapeutics, 1991.

——. True and False Accusations of Child Sex Abuse, Creative Therapeutics, 1992.

Jones Soderman, Jill. The Foundation for Child Victims of the Family Courts. https://fcvfc.org. Many articles on the failures and criminal activities of the family courts.

Appendix

Document 1: Hairbrush Emails

Statement from the mother of the four children for whom I served as a child advocate in bringing charges of physical abuse against the father.

6/13/2005

APPENDIX

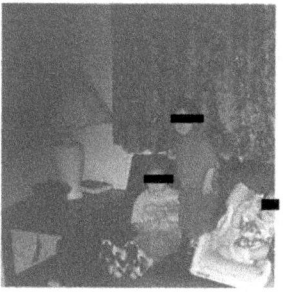

Theopenmind

From: [redacted]
To: "Jill Jones-Soderman" <[redacted]>; "Jill Jones-Soderman" <[redacted]>
Sent: Monday, June 13, 2005 2:55 AM
Attach: [redacted] sitting as guard over the kids with brush in hand--1996.jpg; [redacted]-2-sitting as guard over the kids with brush in hand--1996.jpg; dual judgement of divorce.. March..21..2001.jpg
Subject: FOR YOUR REVIEW

Jill,

Ex-husband 'S' has used it against me that I had spanked our son on his butt with a brush, when he was around 4 years old.

[I know it was wrong and I corrected my discipline tactics to teach my kids the 'right and wrongs' of whatever they do, it is NOT my way to hit out of anger. I also, know that if I teach them that hitting is how to get someone to do what you want, then they will use this tactic in their own lives and with their own children oneday.]

Having said all of that, I am sending you this photo, because as I was saying 'S' has time and time again, tried to say that I was a BAD MOTHER because I had hit my son on his butt with a brush......look at this photo and see the terror & fear in son 's face. Pay attention to where his eyes are focused.....he is staring at the brush in his father's hand, expecting that it will come flying towards him at any second. Tell me what 3 1/2 year old would sit so still, hands crossed, staring at his father's hand holding a brush the way he is unless there is something wrong??? NOT TO MENTION A CHILD WHO IS HYPER-ACTIVE!!

I hope you can see the fear in his face and notice where he is focusing his gaze............troubling isn't it??

By the way I am also sending a copy of my divorce, for whatever it is worth. At a minimum, it will show that I was already divorced when I went to Court for the restraining order with Gloria in 2001. Even though we were VERY RECENTLY divorced [redacted] still didn't keep his distance! As a Muslim this was an extreme violation of the male/female seperation rules of our religion. Not to mention that as an arab/egyptian this kind of behavior was unheard of---amongst non-married adults of the opposite sex----especially ones who were previously married!!

Please respond when you see this email.

--[redacted]

Do you Yahoo!?
Read only the mail you want - Yahoo! Mail SpamGuard.

6/13/2005

APPENDIX

FROM : DANIELLE LOUGH   FAX NO. : 973 237 1718   Aug. 02 2001 03:27PM P1

From: ▮▮▮▮▮▮

8/2/01

DOCTOR,

This is the letter 'S' showed Dashert Gruber presented in ORDER on 7-24-01, from Summer '97. Why did he sit on this info if his concern was so genuine + founded? Why'd he keep this letter all this time, too? Unless it was to hold onto, until he needed it? Not for concern, help, etc.

Document 2: Letter to Investigator Cresenz

JILL SODERMAN, PhD,
MSW, CSW, ACSW, BCCSW, LCSW, NAFC, AFC, CCP

Diplomat in Psychiatric Social Work   Psychotherapist/Psychoanalyst
Forensic Expert

NJ Lic LCSW NO. 04238-LC   NY Lic. CSW No. PRO 13488-1
Certified Domestic Violence Counselor
Diplomat National Association of Forensic Counselors

Tel.
Fax.

July 25, 2001

VIA CERTIFIED MAIL
RETURN RECEIPT REQUESTED

Criminal Investigator Charles Cresenz
Division of Criminal Justice

Attention: Records & Identification

RE: Mother and Sons

Dear Investigator Cresenz:

▬▬▬ and her 3 sons were referred to me, by Strengthen Our Sisters of West Milford, New Jersey, for evaluation for Domestic Abuse and Child Abuse.

The three children (ages 5, 6, and 8 yrs. old) have been seen by me on a weekly basis, for more than 60 hours at this point, in individual and joint treatment. Upon seeing the children individually, on their own, and without coercion, each relayed detailed and complete, from beginning to end, stories of physical and emotional abuse. The oldest child, ▬▬▬, described in detail having his feet tied with a twisted sheet and hung upside down over a door, where his father, ▬▬▬, beat him with a wooden stick and a belt. The two oldest children, described being zipped into a suitcase by their father. Each of the children described their own episodes individually and out of the hearing of their mother. Jointly, they each described episodes of being hit with sticks, slapped and pushed. Each of the children, also, spontaneously stated that they feared for their mothers life and safety, as they stated their father would hit, slap and beat their mother. ▬▬▬, the oldest child, related that he has memories and nightmares of his mother having been beaten with the handle of a hammer in her stomach when she was pregnant with his younger brother. ▬▬▬ expresses intense fear of his father and often screams and cries when his father is mentioned, and he clings to his mother, when in her presence. The younger boys are extremely hyperactive and relate the events described with ridgid smiles on their faces.

APPENDIX

I reported the events of my sessions on April 12, 2001 to the West Milford Police Department and, on the following day, I contacted ▓▓▓▓ of the Division of Youth and Family Services in Paterson, New Jersey.

Further, I accompanied Ms. ▓▓▓ to the Domestic Violence services at Paterson Family Court. We appeared before Judge Marmo along with a neighbor of Ms. ▓▓▓, whom I had contact with, unfortunately, for a period of more than 8 hours and I spent an entire day with the neighbor ▓▓▓ in Court and spent time speaking with her over lunch. As the day progressed, I could observe Ms. ▓▓▓'s demeanor deteriorate over the day. She became more shrunken and her stance; she appeared weary, quiet and suspicious. I learned in the course of the day, mainly at lunch, that Ms. ▓▓▓ had a number of prescribed medications to take. I asked her what medications she was taking and she showed me the bottles and at the point, I realized that she was taking medication for schizophrenia. As the day progressed, I not only realized that Ms. ▓▓▓ suffered from schizophrenia, but, that she also, suffered from paranoid ideation. By the end of the day the person who was originally a reasonably friendly, outgoing person had become withdrawn, slumped over and peered at me sideways as I drove her and my client home to their apartment from Court, when arriving home ▓▓▓▓▓ opened the door and ran into the house.

In Judge Marmo's Court earlier that day the neighbor complemented Ms. ▓▓▓ on being a wonderful loving mother, who was attentive to her children and cared for them very well. She stated that she was in terror of the father ▓▓▓ and she was fearful of testifying on Ms. ▓▓▓'s behalf, because she was fearful of Mr. ▓▓▓. When Ms. ▓▓▓ had to return to Court for a Final Restraining Order, the Judge had instructed her to bring her neighbor with her. Ms. ▓▓▓ was accompanied to Court by a Staff Member from the Domestic Violence Shelter, Strengthen Our Sisters, attorney Bernard Weiss and myself and Ms. ▓▓▓'s children as well. At this court proceeding the neighbor changed her testimony and stated that the mother ▓ was the person of whom she was afraid of and that Mr. ▓▓▓ was a good father. The neighbor stated that Ms. ▓▓▓ had locked her in a room in Ms. ▓▓▓'s apartment. I had visited Ms. ▓▓▓'s apartment with the children to trace steps and events that the children described and noted that the only locks on the bedroom doors were on the inside of the doors. When I learned that the testimony of the neighbor ▓▓▓ was being held against Ms. ▓▓▓ and that bizarre and fanciful and violent fantasies were being provided as testimony and had heard of these events from Mr. Weiss and members of the Domestic Violence Shelter Staff, and wanted the Judge to be aware that, in my professional opinion and experience spent with the neighbor, I would have diagnosed her as being a paranoid schizophrenic and an evaluation should be made of this person's testimony.

Judge McVeigh contacted DYFS to do an immediate evaluation of Ms. ▓▓▓, her children and the home; however, DYFS staff never appeared at Ms. ▓▓▓'s home. As per my personal knowledge, in discussion with DYFS caseworker, Kathy ▓▓▓, she had visited Ms. ▓▓▓'s home and found no evidence of violence or problems with her care of the children. As per the enclosed report, DYFS has stated that they do not want custody of the children and want no part of the case as they have found no basis of child abuse and recommended that the whole family be referred for treatment. Further, DYFS stated that they deferred to the evaluation and recommendation of Paul Dasher, the court appointed psychologist who interviewed the father ▓▓▓ with the two younger children while the oldest child was being hospitalized at St. Clare's Hospital suffering from Post-Traumatic Stress Disorder following the first visit that was ordered by the court using Police force to place the children in the father's car.

It is important to note that Paul Dasher did not extend the same professional courtesy to Ms. ███ regarding interviewing her with the children as part of the court ordered evaluation. The Division of Youth and Family Services are simply following an evaluation of Paul Dasher which is extremely biased, and in total contrast to my reports and evaluations, having spent much more time with these children. He referred the custody of the children be transferred to the father and no contact by Ms. ███ which maybe putting children in extreme danger. Also, the children have been forced to cease treatment with me, so they now feel they have no ally or outlet to express their feelings. This is despite the fact that I have informed DYFS of the deleterious effects on the children. It is also my understanding to date from other therapeutic personal that the children exhibit homocidal and suicidal behaviors at times and articulate such thoughts as well. The two younger boys are acutely hyperactive, which they were not, while in treatment with me. All three children were extremely traumatized after their initial encounter with Paul Dasher, when they spoke of the evaluation they would cry and cling to their mother and was this way for the entire weekend and remained such until Monday morning when I had session with the mother and 3 children.

Following the initial hearing before Judge McVeigh, Judge ███'s McVeigh recused herself from the case and Bernard Weiss, Ms. ███'s attorney, withdrew from the case as well, leaving Ms. ███ with no attorney to represent her, while her former husband was represented by private counsel. Numerous attempts by Ms. ███ and myself to procure an attorney were in vain. Ms. ███ and I went through the list of agencies which provide pro bono and sliding scale services and were constantly told that the case was too complicated for them to take on. Ms. ███ has also, contacted the Passaic County Bar Association and is attempting to find a lawyer thru the bar association.

As to Ms. ███, I do not wish to portray her as a perfect person without any foibles of her own. However, it has been consistantly Ms. ███ who has sought treatment for herself and her children, not Mr. ███ who has, instead forced visitation with children who had feared him and did not wish to visit with him. To my knowledge, Mr. ███ never requested any type of therapeutic intervention to deal with his children, who expressed fear of him and rejection of him. Subsequent to the divorce, the children were prepared by their mother for visitation with their father. She always made the children available with an overnight bag packed, for the children to join their father for visitation. The police were present when the children stated in front of their father and in front of the police that they did not wish to go on a visitation with their father; that they feared him and did not wish to go in his car. When Mr. ███ met with their resistance, Mr. ███ went to Court and obtained a Court Order(a copy of which is enclosed) requiring the police to use whatever force necessary to place the children in the father's car. On the first day of this court-ordered visitation, I was on the telephone with Ms. ███, as she was on the street with the police, the children were crying and refusing to go with their father. The children were running from the police and the police pursued the eldest child in their police car. I could hear on the telephone that the oldest son, ███ was screaming and Ms. ███ wailing. As the police approached ███ in their car he sat down on the street and was holding his head and rocking back and forth as per description of Ms. ███, as she was moving toward her son. As the police officer forcibly picked ███ up, I could hear him, ███ yelling "NO!!" repeatedly, stating "he beats me up, I dont want to go with him." and pleading with his mother, "Mommy, I dont wanna' go" and "Mommy, dont let them take me." The police officer, whom I could hear said to ███, "come on, be a man." I was on the telephone with Ms. ███ as she was running around the street and neighborhood behind her children pleading with the police officers not to do this.

APPENDIX

As per report by Ms. ■■, Mr. ■■■■■■ arrived in his taxicab with another man, it is my understanding from the children that this man held them in the car to restrain them from exiting the vehicle to go to their mother. In addition, it is my understanding from the children this man spent the night sleeping in their father's home and slept on the living room floor blocking the apartment door. I suspect, to keep the children from running away.

I gather that during the visit Mr. ■■■■■■ treated the children reasonably well, with the exception of, the eldest son described to me how his father made him sit up all night as a punishment for making his younger brother crash on his bicycle. He went on to explain that every time he would begin to doze off his father would hit him with a wooden spoon to jar him awake, and that when (as the child describes it) it became daylight the father then allowed him to go to sleep.

In my professional opinion, Ms. ■■■ suffers from Battered Women's Syndrome which places her at a disadvantage when it comes to adequately articulating her situation and defending herself. She is a mother who has 3 children who, in my professional opinion, suffer from ADHD and PTSD. I have seen her for more than 60 hours since April 12, 2001. I have seen the children for an equal amount of time, in individual and joint sessions. I have found Ms. ■■■ to be totally honest with respect to her own history and her dealings with her children. Under no circumstance have I saw her as an abusive parent with respect to her report and the report of the children.

Over the weekend of July 20th, 2001, Mr. ■■■■■■■ took the 2 youngest children for the Court-Ordered Friday-Saturday overnight visitation. I must note the oldest child was hospitalized at St. Clare's Hospital following the first visitation, due to PTSD. On Saturday when the children were to be returned to their mother's residence, Mr. ■■■■■■ did not return the children. Ms. ■■■ was escorted by the Elizabeth police to Mr. ■■■■■■'s apartment. After a few moments discussion with Mr. ■■■■■■, the police joined Ms. ■■■ curbside where they had asked her to wait since there is a TRO. While their backs were turned speaking to Ms. ■■■, Mr. ■■■■■■ was seen by a woman accompanying Ms. ■■■ running to the parking lot carrying a child fitting one of Ms. ■■■'s sons' description. When the EPD went to check on Mr. ■■■■■■'s whereabouts and to inform him to stay put for DYFS to be called, the police found that Mr. ■■■■■■ had in fact fled in his Newark taxicab which had been parked in the parking lot on the apartment complex premises just prior to that. It is my understanding as reported to me by Ms. ■■■, that when she insisted that DYFS be called to the scene to assess the situation, she was told there was nothing the EPD could do as the children were no longer available, and to go home and contact the Court or DYFS case worker Monday morning. The problem with this situation is the court order and accompanying paperwork made available to the police officers by both Ms. ■■■ and Mr. ■■■■■■, did not allow or inform the Elizabeth Police to determine the children should remain with the father, and this is what they were informing Ms. ■■■ of,(that they were allowing him to keep the boys in his care), when their backs were turned and Mr. ■■■■■■ fled with the 2 young boys. Mr. ■■■■■■ could have been out of the country and on his way to Egypt by Monday, not to mention the boys could have been put in a very unhealthy and/or unsafe situation for that period of time.

In closing, I wish to state that this is a very abbreviated summary of numerous and complex events. I have annexed collateral reports to give you a sense of the vicious, prejudicial and inattentive unjust behavior of the Court and DYFS in dealing with Ms. ■■■'s situation. In my professional opinion, Ms. ■■■ has been slandered, as well as poorly represented and moreso misrepresented.

Testimony from myself, St. Clare's Hospital and Dr. Kennedy has not been permitted to be presented to the Court, only a report of Paul Dasher has been allowed to be presented, and this report, as per my understanding in unfavorable to Ms. ▮▮▮▮, I, myself have been threatened by ▮▮▮▮'s attorney, Richard Gruber, that if I do not cease my support and treatment of Ms. ▮▮▮▮, that "there will be all kinds of collateral litigation" against me and that he is recommending that I be investigated by the prosecutor's office, as Mr. Gruber plans to state that I have instructed Ms. ▮▮▮▮ in how to brainwash the children and have thus caused her to bring a restraining order against Mr. ▮▮▮▮ and have caused her to instruct the children in stating that they were abused by their father. Mr. Gruber stated that he intended to discredit my report and that I am the "target" to be eliminated.

I have contacted the Ethics Committee of the New Jersey Bar Association, Essex County, to indicate that, as a witness, I have been threatened in the course of performing my moral and ethical responsibilities as a fully licensed professional and basically told to disappear. I have also, contacted with Ms. ▮▮▮▮, the Executive Director of DYFS to report the circumstances of slander and liable that have been directed against Ms. ▮▮▮▮ in an attempt to remove her children from her.

I would appreciate any assistance or advice that you can provide. Please feel free to contact me at ▮▮▮▮▮▮▮▮

Very Truly Yours,

Jill Soderman

Jill Soderman,

Document 3: Note to Paul Dasher

This is the handwritten note I gave to Paul Dasher, PhD, in the court hallway during a hearing at which Dasher reputedly appeared before Judge Margaret Mary McVeigh. (I was not present in that courtroom scene.) Dasher then gave this handwritten note to Judge Margaret Mary McVeigh, who called it a "report to the court" from me. The fabricated communication provided by Margaret Mary McVeigh to the New Jersey Licensing Board was part of a contrived complaint related to events that never occurred that were then used as the basis for investigation against my New Jersey social work license.

4/8/2001

To Dr. Paul Dasher

From Dr Jill Soderman

Re: Harassment and abuse of [redacted] and her three sons

Attached is a brief note to the court with regard to material of which I am aware re: the abuse of these three children & their fear and dislike of their father.

never left alone at any time and that they are attended by a friend of [the mother] if she is away from home for work. However, the children are fearful about giving out the name(s) of their caretakers as they fear that their father will "hurt" whomever attempts to assist [the mother] and the children.

Of note is that as soon as I returned from court with [the mother] I began receiving numerous strange phone calls of men speaking in hushed tones – heavy breathing and moments of silence – I received approximately a dozen calls the first evening when I returned from court. When I stated that the calls were being recorded and traced – they reduced in number – . I still received an occasional bizarre call – a situation I never experience in the past –

As noted – I have attended court with [the mother] on the two occasions for restraining orders – once with Judge Marmar – and the second time with Judge McVeigh – who refused to see the children in chambers or to assign a guardian ad litem for their protection – Her solution to conflicting testimony from a Puerto Rican schizophrenic former shelter inhabitant and current neighbor of [the mother] was to recommend that the children be placed in foster care until Dyfus could evaluate the situation – Dyfus had never returned the judge's call – so the case was referred to you –

I would consider any separation of the children from their mother utterly outrageous and an egregious and destructive error on the court's part. If I can be of further help – please call me at [redacted] JS

Document 4: Margaret McVeigh Letter to Court

A letter from Judge Mary Margaret McVeigh to the courts about the note to Paul Dasher.

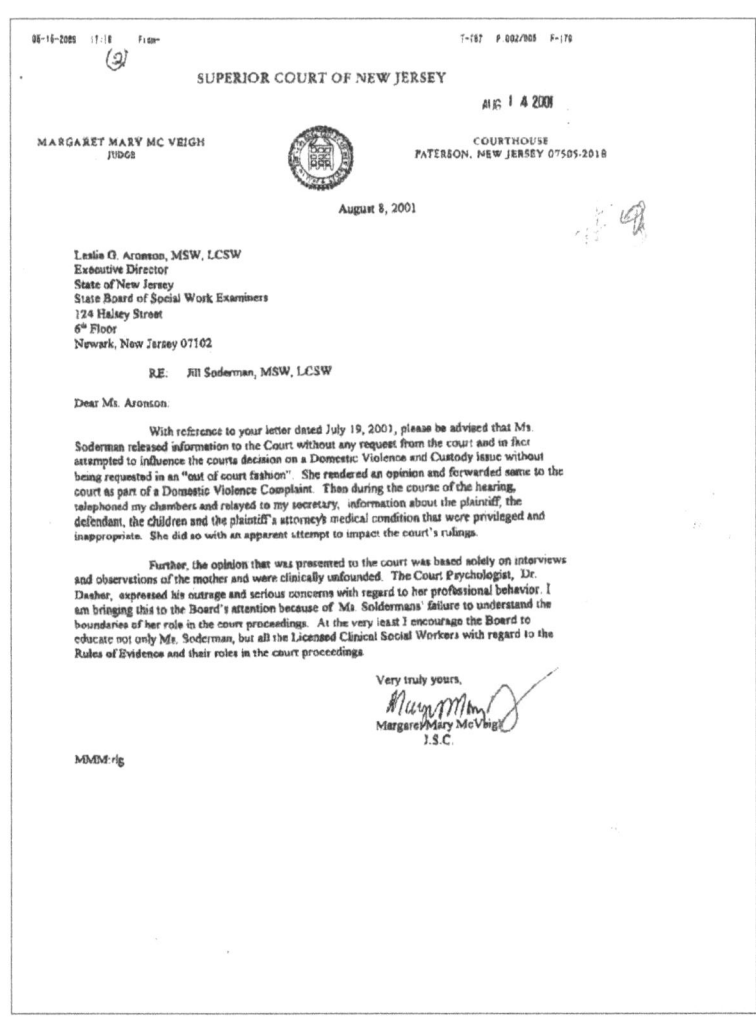

Document 5: Custody Order

```
                                              06/22/97  12:28am  P. 002


RICHARD L. GRUBER, ESQ.                          FILED
One Riverfront Plaza, Suite 500
Newark, New Jersey 07102                        JUN 2 7 2001
Tel. (973) 624-3999
Fax (973) 824-2255                        GLENN R. WENZEL, J.S.C.
Attorney for Defendant ▓▓▓▓▓▓▓▓▓

    THE MOTHER              SUPERIOR COURT OF NEW JERSEY
                            CHANCERY DIVISION – FAMILY PART
                Plaintiff,  PASSAIC COUNTY
       v.                   Docket No. FM-16-623-00
    THE FATHER                       FV- 16-002197-01
                                      Civil Action
                Defendant,            ORDER
```

This matter having been opened to the Court by Richard L. Gruber, Esq., attorney for Defendant, ▓▓▓, and upon notice to ▓▓▓, pro se, and the Court having reviewed the moving papers and having heard arguments of counsel, and

WHEREAS on this Court on June 4, 2001 entered an Order granting the Defendant parenting time with his three minor children, ▓▓, ▓▓▓ and ▓▓▓, every week from Friday at 5:00 p.m. until Saturday at 5:00 p.m. to be picked up by the Defendant curbside in front of Plaintiff's residence; and

WHEREAS the Plaintiff has failed to permit said parenting time;

IT IS ON THIS 27 DAY OF JUNE, 2001,

ORDERED that the Defendant shall have parenting time with the three minor children from 5:00 p.m. Friday until 5:00p.m. Saturday every week, and it is further

ORDERED that the police shall render any and all assistance necessary to effectuate the parenting time as set forth in this Order, and it is further

ORDERED that failure of the Plaintiff to comply with the terms of this Order shall result in alternative custody arrangements for the three minor children, and it is further

ORDERED that Defendant counsel shall submit a certification for fees associated with the filing of this motion for aid of litigants rights, and it is further

ORDERED that a copy of this Order be served on the Plaintiff immediately by certified mail return receipt requested.

                                         Glenn R. Wenzel, J.S.C.

Document 6: St. Claire's Letter

```
5462747  MR#002219701 8Y
KENNEDY, PAUL
RC 1210-B ELKARYONEY, 161.
```

Saint Clare's Hospital

July 13, 2001

Candy Pasca, Supervisor
Division of Youth and Family Services
Northern Passaic County District Office
100 Hamilton Plaza, 11th Floor
Paterson, NJ 07505

Re: ▮▮▮▮▮ D.O.B: 6/17/93

Ms. Pasca:

▮▮▮▮ is an eight year old child who was admitted to St. Clares Children's Crisis Intervention Service, a children's inpatient psychiatric unit, via the emergency room of St. Mary's Hospital on 7/7/01. He was brought to the emergency room for significant acting - out behavior at school. My sources of information are direct interviews with the child, his mother, and written reports from his school and from Jill Soderman Ph. D., his therapist.

The letter from his school, dated 5/31/01, describes a deterioration in his behavior at that time. His behavior was consistent with someone who had been physically abused. Dr. Soderman had evaluated the children and their mother and described in her reports her opinion that the children and their mother had been the victims of abuse by ▮▮▮'s father and she advised that his parental rights be terminated. Interviews with ▮▮▮'s mother confirmed a history of domestic violence in her marriage in addition to physical abuse of the children by her ex-husband, Mr. ▮▮▮▮. Recently, the Court ordered overnight unsupervised visitation for Mr. ▮▮▮▮ with his children. The local police went with the father to enforce the order and ▮▮▮ was forced to go in spite of his protests.

I have interviewed ▮▮▮ several times over the past week. Our trained staff work with the patients twenty four hours a day. ▮▮▮ is receiving medication for symptoms of Attention Deficit Hyperactive Disorder. He is quite explicit about his fear of his father. He talks about being hit by his father with "sticks," and hit while tied by his feet and hung up - side - down over a door. He says that his father hit his two younger siblings. He describes bad dreams and flashbacks which are memories of this abuse which is consistent with a diagnosis of Post Traumatic Stress Disorder

[1] 30 Powerville Road, Boonton Township, New Jersey 07005-8701

Because of these memories, ▓▓ does not want to visit with his father. His feelings about his father are expressed in the absence of his mother and appear to be based on his experience and he does not appear to be repeating something he has been told to say by his mother.

It is my professional opinion that ▓▓ has diagnoses of Attention Deficit Disorder and Post Traumatic Stress Disorder. His allegations of abuse should be investigated by the Division of Youth and Family Services. It would be severely harmful to his mental health for him to be forced to have contact with his father who he continues to fear.

Sincerely,

Paul V. Kennedy M.D.
Board Certified Child and Adult Psychiatry
Clinical Assistant Professor U.M.D.N.J.

Document 7: Letter from Strengthen Our Sisters

In which the director provided testimony related to her direct knowledge of severe physical emotional sexual abuse of shelter resident/mother of three boys who had become the subjects of my advocacy.

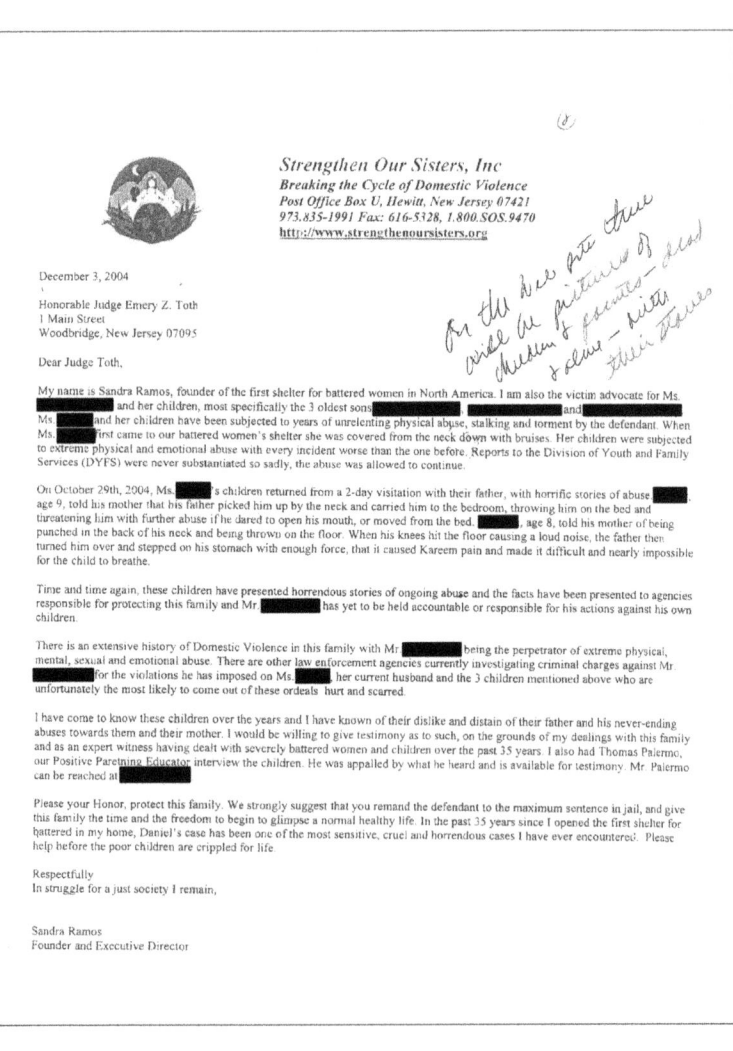

Document 8: Press Release

12 Year Old Boy Kills Himself When Court Mandates Visit With Abusive Father – Mother Wants His Memory to Have Meaning Towards Changing the System

On Tuesday, October 25, 2005, ▓▓▓▓▓, a twelve year old boy hung himself, choosing death over the prospect of a court mandated visitation with his father. The tragedy of his death is overshadowed by the tragedy of his life, which was fraught with violence at the hands of an abusive father and the unwillingness of the courts to protect him.

According to his mother's advocate, Sandra Ramos, who is the Founder and Executive Director of Strengthen Our Sisters shelter for battered women and children, ▓▓▓▓▓ and her three young sons lived in terror for several years. Not only were the children subjected to witnessing their mother being brutally beaten repeatedly by their father, but they were themselves were victims of his wild abuse. In August of 1998, ▓▓▓▓▓ confided with a friend that she feared for her children's lives, after her oldest son Islam had been hung upside down in a twisted sheet and beaten with a stick on the bottoms of his feet by his father. Her friend called Sandra Ramos and Strengthen Our Sisters took in the distraught mother and her children. Shortly after their arrival to the shelter, ▓▓▓▓▓ applied for and was granted a restraining order and believed she and her children would finally be protected. However, an appeal was filed by the father and the court ordered unsupervised visitation, despite ▓▓▓▓▓'s pleas to have these visits monitored.

All too often, the children would come back from the visitations with bumps and bruises, obviously disturbed and begging not to have to go again. This went on for years. ▓▓▓▓▓ would petition the courts seeking help for her children, showing photographs of the bruises and would request supervised visitation, which would be granted but then always overturned when the father and his expensive attorney would go to the court and protest. At one point ▓▓▓▓▓, at the age of 8, who was the recipient of the most extreme abuse, experienced a breakdown and spent 19 days at St. Clare's Hospital in Denville, NJ. The psychiatrist's report to the court stated ▓▓▓▓▓ was experiencing post-traumatic stress disorder, attention deficit disorder, and extreme depression from the abuse he had experienced and witnessed over the years.

Finally, in May 2005, the judge mandated psychiatric evaluations for the entire family to determine whether the children should be forced to continue visitations with their father. ▓▓▓▓▓ and her three sons heartily embraced this opportunity to have someone finally understand what they had endured and present their evaluations to the court. However, the father left the country and did not return for five months. During this time, he was served with contempt papers for failing to comply with the ordered psychological evaluation. His excuse was that he had only expected to be gone for two weeks, to tend to his ailing mother (who according to ▓▓▓▓▓ he had previously declared dead to the INS in 1994, when he wanted to leave the country and be able to return), but that he had been further delayed due to a car accident. He had also testified in another courtroom, two weeks prior to leaving the country, that he was anxious to get the evaluation over with, as he was planning on being away for several months. On July 18, 2005 the judge called the family back into court to assess the evaluations, but since the father was still in Egypt, he ordered his parenting visitation time suspended, stating his reasons were based on the father's contempt, and on his assessment and review of the psychiatrist letter to the court. This letter stated the children had clearly been subjected to abuse and that they should be able to make their own choices about visitation. The letter also stated that the judges formal recommendation would take place after he actually had the opportunity to meet with the father.

On September 8, 2005, the father asked the judge to vacate the order of July 18, 2005, at which time the judge stated he would review all orders and documentation on October 21, 2005.

After leaving the shelter, ▮▮▮▮ met and married her current husband and gave birth to another son. ▮▮▮▮, her husband and her children longed to move away from the area and go to Kansas where she had grown up, and where there were supportive relatives. On October 7, 2005, ▮▮▮▮ put in a request to the court to relocate with children to Kansas City, at which time the judge arbitrarily vacated the July 18, 2005 order and mandated supervised visitation for the father, despite the fact that he did not yet have a full report. ▮▮▮▮'s attorney protested and said that no visitation should be granted until the court had the full psychiatric profile of the father. The judge denied his appeal.

▮▮▮▮ reported that when she broke the news to her children that they would have to see their father, she assured them that the visit would be supervised. The two younger boys protested but then reluctantly agreed. ▮▮▮▮; however, was beside himself and kept saying that they can't make me see him. She said he was extremely agitated over the next few days, so she called the psychiatrist's office to ask that he intervene and make an appeal to the judge, on behalf of her son. Regrettably, before any of this could happen, ▮▮▮▮ went into his room the next day and hung himself, choosing death over the prospects of being forced to be with his torturer.

Hesia Rosenberg, Director of the Circle of Life Organization, has been working tirelessly to help make the public more aware of what the courts are not doing to protect children like ▮▮▮▮. "I have received letters from Florida to Washington, Texas and Tennessee and they continue to pour in. New Jersey is not an isolated state when it comes to corruption. All states are amassed with judicial and legal corruption, and we have to stop it." She recommended that people watch a new PBS documentary scheduled to air on November 20, 2005, entitled "Breaking the Silence", to educate themselves on this national scandal of how the courts are neglecting their duty to protect our most vulnerable, abused women and children.

In 2000, Jill Soderman was a volunteer at Strengthen Our Sisters. She was a licensed therapist and clinical social worker, having over 33 years experience as a non-biased expert witness in many domestic violence cases in New York and New Jersey. Jill attempted to intervene, on behalf of ▮▮▮▮'s children, after interviewing them in the presence of their father. She reported to the court at that time that she felt the children were in grave danger. After reporting such, Jill was harassed on a daily basis by receiving hundreds of phone calls with male voices, muttering in a language she did not understand. This harassment continued, as she persisted in trying to get help for the children, when her house suddenly burned down. Though the perpetrator was never found, she was told by police and firemen that it had clearly been a case of arson. Ironically, the house where ▇▇▇ and her children lived was also burned down.

Jill Soderman is currently involved in a second doctoral program involving forensic evaluation and psychoanalysis cases, with particular emphasis on the role of the expert witness. She originally saw the children with ▇▇▇, while they were residing at the shelter and had lined up many witnesses, such as teachers and principles, as well as friends. Jill was never allowed to testify in court, nor was her witnesses, some of whom claimed to have been threatened as well. Instead, she was discredited and so was ▇▇▇ by a court appointed evaluator, who claimed that the children had been brainwashed. According to Jill, this evaluator remained a protagonist of the father throughout many of the court hearings, though he was never subpoenaed. It was his claims that brought the Division of Youth and Family Services (DYFS) into the case. DYFS did not want to accept custody of the children and so transferred custody to the father, who brought them back to their mother after three weeks, claiming they were incorrigible. It was at this time that ▇▇▇ had a breakdown and was brought to St. Clare's Hospital in Denville, NJ, claiming that he and his brothers had been beaten and brutalized by his father, while in his care.

Jill claims she was convinced she had to help the children after her extended interview with them. In the presence of their father, he would read the Koran aloud while the children talked to Jill about the abuse, which included being put into suitcases and beaten. On one occasion, she witnessed their mother bringing them for a mandated weekend visit with their father, who was waiting in a car outside with another woman. When the children saw him, they ran in all different directions, screaming that they did not want to go with him. The father then called the police and because of the court ordered documentation, the police had no choice but to chase the children through the streets and force them into the car with their father. Jill said that one of the policemen commented that the event should have been video tapped and presented to a judge. At that time the children were ages four, five and six.

Bereft and distraught with grief over the loss of her son, ▇▇▇ requested that ▇▇▇'s father not be present at the funeral but to be permitted to visit the mosque at a private time. The same judge who ordered the dreaded visitation said he would put in an order to suspend visitation with the other two children. However, a new judge stepped in to take over the case and said the father would be allowed full participation in the funeral.

▇▇▇ also stated that she wants the memory of her son to mean something. She wants the court to be held accountable, so that the tragedy of ▇▇▇'s life and his death will inspire others into action, in order to protect other children from the same fate. She said the judges and the courts had all the information before them. "They must be exposed because they dropped the ball and now my son is dead."

Those wishing to help can send tax-deductible donations toward desperately needed funeral expenses to Strengthen Our Sisters, marking the envelope "███ Fund" and send to POB U, Hewitt, NJ. People wishing further information or who wish to share their own stories can contact the Circle of Life Organization at 908-362-9526 or Strengthen Our Sisters at 973-728-0777 and ask for Sandra Ramos.

**12 Year Old Boy Kills Himself When Court Mandates Visit With Abusive Father –
Mother Wants His Memory to Have Meaning Towards Changing the System**

On Tuesday, October 25, 2005, Islam Elkaryoncy, a twelve year old boy hung himself, choosing death over the prospect of a court mandated visitation with his father. The tragedy of his death is overshadowed by the tragedy of his life, which was fraught with violence at the hands of an abusive father and the unwillingness of the courts to protect him.

According to Danielle Lough's advocate, Sandra Ramos, who is the Founder and Executive Director of Strengthen Our Sisters shelter for battered women and children, Danielle and her three young sons lived in terror for several years. Not only were the children subjected to witnessing their mother being brutally beaten repeatedly by their father, but they were themselves were victims of his wild abuse. In August of 1998, Danielle confided with a friend that she feared for her children's lives, after her oldest son Islam had been hung upside down in a twisted sheet and beaten with a stick on the bottoms of his feet by his father. Her friend called Sandra Ramos and Strengthen Our Sisters took in the distraught mother and her children. Shortly after their arrival to the shelter, Danielle applied for and was granted a restraining order and believed she and her children would finally be protected. However, an appeal was filed by the father and the court ordered unsupervised visitation, despite Danielle's pleas to have these visits monitored.

All too often, the children would come back from the visitations with bumps and bruises, obviously disturbed and begging not to have to go again. This went on for years. Danielle would petition the courts seeking help for her children, showing photographs of the bruises and would request supervised visitation, which would be granted but then always overturned when the father and his expensive attorney would go to the court and protest. At one point Islam, at the age of 8, who was the recipient of the most extreme abuse, experienced a breakdown and spent 19 days at St. Clare's Hospital in Denville, NJ. The psychiatrist's report to the court stated Islam was experiencing post-traumatic stress disorder, attention deficit disorder, and extreme depression from the abuse he had experienced and witnessed over the years.

Finally, in May 2005, the judge mandated psychiatric evaluations for the entire family to determine whether the children should be forced to continue visitations with their father. Danielle and her three sons heartily embraced this opportunity to have someone finally understand what they had endured and present their evaluations to the court. However, the father left the country and did not return for five months. During this time, he was served with contempt papers for failing to comply with the ordered psychological evaluation. His excuse was that he had only expected to be gone for two weeks, to tend to his ailing mother (who according to Danielle he had previously declared dead to the INS in 1994, when he wanted to leave the country and be able to return), but that he had been further delayed due to a car accident. He had also testified in another courtroom, two weeks prior to leaving the country, that he was anxious to get the evaluation over with, as he was planning on being away for several months. On July 18, 2005 the judge were in grave danger. After reporting such, Jill was harassed on a daily basis by receiving hundreds of phone calls with male voices, muttering in a language she did not understand. This harassment continued, as she persisted in trying to get help for the children, when her house suddenly burned down. Though the perpetrator was never found, she was told by police and firemen that it had clearly been a case of arson. Ironically, the house where Danielle and her children lived was also burned down.

Jill Soderman is currently involved in a second doctoral program involving forensic evaluation and psychoanalysis cases, with particular emphasis on the role of the expert witness. She originally saw the children with Danielle, while they were residing at the shelter and had lined up many witnesses, such as teachers and principles, as well as friends. Jill was never allowed to testify in court, nor was her witnesses, some of whom claimed to have been threatened as well. Instead, she was discredited and so was Danielle by a court appointed evaluator, who claimed that the children had been brainwashed. According to Jill, this evaluator remained a protagonist of the father throughout many of the court hearings, though he was never subpoenaed. It was his claims that brought the Division of Youth and Family Services (DYFS) into the case. DYFS did not want to accept custody of the children and so transferred custody to the father, who brought them back to their mother after three weeks, claiming they were incorrigible. It was at this time that Islam had a breakdown and was brought to St. Clare's Hospital in Denville, NJ, claiming that he and his brothers had been beaten and brutalized by his father, while in his care.

Jill claims she was convinced she had to help the children after her extended interview with them. In the presence of their father, he would read the Koran aloud while the children talked to Jill about the abuse, which included being put into suitcases and beaten. On one occasion, she witnessed their mother bringing them for a mandated weekend visit with their father, who was waiting in a car outside with another man. When the children saw him, they ran in all different directions, screaming that they did not want to go with him. The father then called the police and because of the court ordered documentation, the police had no choice but to chase the children through the streets and force them into the car with their father. Jill said that one of the policemen commented that the event should have been video tapped and presented to a judge. At that time the children were ages four, five and six.

Bereft and distraught with grief over the loss of her son, Danielle requested that Islam's father not be present at the funeral but to be permitted to visit the mosque at a private time. The same judge who ordered the dreaded visitation said he would put in an order to suspend visitation with the other two children. However, a new judge stepped in to take over the case and said the father would be allowed full participation in the funeral.

Danielle also stated that she wants the memory of her son to mean something. She wants the court to be held accountable, so that the tragedy of Islam's life and his death will inspire others into action, in order to protect other children from the same fate. She said the judges and the courts had all the information before them. "They must be exposed because they dropped the ball and now my son is dead."

called the family back into court to assess the evaluations, but since the father was still in Egypt, he ordered his parenting visitation time suspended, stating his reasons were based on the father's contempt, and on his assessment and review of the psychiatrist letter to the court. This letter stated the children had clearly been subjected to abuse and that they should be able to make their own choices about visitation. The letter also stated that the judges formal recommendation would take place after he actually had the opportunity to meet with the father.

On September 8, 2005, the father asked the judge to vacate the order of July 18, 2005, at which time the judge stated he would review all orders and documentation on October 21, 2005.

After leaving the shelter, Danielle met and married her current husband and gave birth to another son. Danielle, her husband and her children longed to move away from the area and go to Kansas where Danielle had grown up, and where there were supportive relatives. On October 7, 2005, Danielle put in a request to the court to relocate with children to Kansas City, at which time the judge arbitrarily vacated the July 18, 2005 order and mandated supervised visitation for the father, despite the fact that he did not yet have a full report. Danielle's attorney protested and said that no visitation should be granted until the court had the full psychiatric profile of the father. The judge denied his appeal.

Danielle reported that when she broke the news to her children that they would have to see their father, she assured them that the visit would be supervised. The two younger boys protested but then reluctantly agreed. Islam; however, was beside himself and kept saying that they can't make me see him. She said he was extremely agitated over the next few days, so she called the psychiatrist's office to ask that he intervene and make an appeal to the judge, on behalf of her son. Regrettably, before any of this could happen, Islam went into his room the next day and hung himself, choosing death over the prospects of being forced to be with his torturer.

Hesia Rosenberg, Director of the Circle of Life Organization, has been working tirelessly to help make the public more aware of what the courts are not doing to protect children like Islam. "I have received letters from Florida to Washington, Texas and Tennessee and they continue to pour in. New Jersey is not an isolated state when it comes to corruption. All states are amassed with judicial and legal corruption, and we have to stop it." She recommended that people watch a new PBS documentary scheduled to air on November 20, 2005, entitled "Breaking the Silence", to educate themselves on this national scandal of how the courts are neglecting their duty to protect our most vulnerable, abused women and children.

In 2000, Jill Soderman was a volunteer at Strengthen Our Sisters. She was a licensed therapist and clinical social worker, having over 33 years experience as a non-biased expert witness in many domestic violence cases in New York and New Jersey. Jill attempted to intervene, on behalf of Danielle's children, after interviewing them in the presence of their father. She reported to the court at that time that she felt the children

Those wishing to help can send tax-deductible donations toward desperately needed funeral expenses to Strengthen Our Sisters, marking the envelope "Islam Fund" and send to POB U, Hewitt, NJ. People wishing further information or who wish to share their own stories can contact the Circle of Life Organization at 908-362-9526 or Strengthen Our Sisters at 973-728-0777 and ask for Sandra Ramos.

APPENDIX 267

Document 9: Families in Transition Article

An article in the Daily Record 'Taking the Pain Out of Divorce' about the Families in Transition program.

WHAT'S OLD IS NEW – THE SHADOW OF A GOOD MEMORY

PARENT COORDINATION – AN IDEA PUT INTO EFFECT BY FAMILIES IN TRANSITION – A 5013C NON PROFIT DEVELOPED BY THERESE AMBROSINO AS OF EARLY 2000 WITH THE CLOSE COLLABORATION OF JILL JONES-SODERMAN OF OAK RIDGE NEW JERSEY HAS BEEN REDISCOVERED AS A "UNIQUE" CONSTRUCTIVE TOOL IN DEALING WITH HIGH CONFLICT DIVORCE SITUATIONS.

THE PARENT COORDINATOR ROLE AS CONCEIVED BY JONES-SODERMAN A PSYCHOTHERAPIST FAMILY THERAPIST KNITTED TOGETHER FAMILY THERAPY, MEDIATION – THE CAUCUS INTERVENTION – MEETING WITH ONE MEBER OF THE MEDIATION IN PROCESS WHEN CONFLICT WAS ENTERING A HIGH CONFLICT PHASE AND FAMILY ACCESS TO THE PARENT COORDINATOR SEVEN DAYS PER WEEK/24 HOURS PER DAY.
THE TECHNIQUE PROVED TO BE HIGHLY SUCCESSFUL DEFINED IN TERMS OF KEEPING WARRING PARTNERS OUT OF COURT. A LARGE BODY OF CLIENTS RAPIDLY DEVELOPED AS THE CLIENTELLE OF "FAMILIES IN TRANSITION", 501C3 NON PROFIT LOCATED IN BRANCHVILLE, NJ BETWEEN 2000 AND 2005 BECAME AN ORGANIZATION THAT WAS ADOPTED BY THE SUSSEX COUNTY FAMILY COURT AS A SOURCE OF REFERRALS FOR FAMILIES IN CONFLICT .

SEMINARS HELD AT AND PROMOTED BY NEWTON MEMORIAL HOSPITAL

FEATURED JILL JONES- SODERMAN, AMONG OTHER SPEAKERS DEALING WITH SUCH TOPICS AS THE IMPACT OF HIGH CONFLICT ON CHILDREN AND DIVORCING PARTNERS, THE DIAGNOSIS AND TREATMENT OF PARENTAL ALIENATION DISCUSSED AS A DYNAMIC IN INTERPERSONAL ABUSE – PARENTS TOWARD CHILDREN/ CHILDREN WITH PARENTS. THE FAMILY RESOLUTION CENTER IN NYACK NEW YORK NOW CARRRIES ON THE EXCELLENT WORK ETHICS, SPEAKING, WRITING, INDIVIDUAL/FAMILY TREATMENT, THERAPEUTIC MEDIATION AND PARENT COORDINATOR SERVICES BEGUN YEARS AGO IN BRANCHVILLE NEW JERSEY.

WHAT IS OLD MAY BECOME NEW AGAIN, BUR A GOOD IDEA NEVER DIES IT JUST TRANSFORMS OVER TIME AND SPACE.

Document 10: Dr. Monty Weinstein Recommendation

DR. MONTY WEINSTEIN, PSY.D, M.P.A., D.A.P.A AND N.C.P.
FOUNDER AND DIRECTOR OF THE FAMILY THERAPY CENTER OF
NEW YORK AND GEORGIA

AUG. 10, 2012

RE: JILL JONES-SODERMAN MSW, PHD, MSHS

I am Dr. Weinstein, Psy.D. M.P.A, D.A.P.A.,, and N.C.P. My more than fifty years of uninterrupted, widely documented practice includes clinical treatment, expert witness testimony and numerous areas of work documented on my web site THEFAMILYTHERAPYCENTER OF NEW YORK AND GROEGIA.COM

My reputation is unblemished as a vocal, unrelenting advocate against the abuses of bureaucrats who attempt to manipulate clinical, administrative, psychologically toxic diagnoses to discredit professionals. I am well aware of the abuses of the administrative licensing board bureaucrats who seek to seek to join forces with the large pharmaceutical companies, the draconian control exercised by the division of so called child protective services and the attempt by licensing boards to recruit members who are obedient as opposed to educated, independent, outspoken, ethical professionals.

The unrestrained actions of the courts and their minions have removed the licenses of all too many independent, professionals who are clinically ethical as well as astute, thus creating a dangerously biased and frequently corrupt court system basing case rulings not on law, but on manipulation of, or pandering to power and control.

1

The iron hand of the various administrative licensing boards are extending from the clinical divisions to those of law and medicine, demanding members follow practices which may often require obedience to highly suspect practices. Threats to those who challenge authority are being called into question with demands for them to be subject to psychiatric evaluations which most often result in the loss of their licenses and the destruction of their credibility and ability to work in any field related to their area of expertise. Young lawyers who have passed the bar exam, who have an activist history of suing judges or lawyers are being kept from admission to the bar associations that they should be allowed to join, in order to proceed with their professions.

We are finding that mandated reporters, expected to report child neglect, abuse, sexual abuse are being accused of issuing false reports, when in fact the evidence is beyond clear and convincing. Those who are refusing to diagnose mentally healthy elders as needing to be placed into the care of legal conservator ships, managed by attorneys who often drain the inheritances of those who were meant to receive the benefits bequeathed are being called before licensing boards, having demands to submit to psychiatric/psychological exams which are then used as probable cause for professionals to lose their licenses.

Because of the multiple egregious acts by the state, courts, judges, licensing boards, jealous peers, with all of whom I am fully familiar, having been similarly subjected to attempts at attack, unsuccessfully, I am writing this statement of support for

2

Jill Jones-Soderman, MSW, psychiatric social worker, PHD Psychoanalyst, MSHS masters in law and expert witness testimony. Jill Jones-Soderman has actively published, defended and treated the complex of controversial cases noted, for which she has earned the enmity of the licensing boards who have confabulated charges against her which have no value or merit and include no patient complaints. In fact, the complaints by the boards have been generated because of her success in the courts as a forensic advocate.

Jill Jones has been a colleague and co worker on many cases over the past six years. We have spent many hours discussing clinical work, writing, working together in various forms of advocacy and working on various elements of cases together. She is well liked by her clients, particularly because of her expertise and propensity to prevail in difficult cases despite the threats from authorities or opposing parties. Threats without probable cause have been confronted by her, but she would have to walk on water to prevail against false charges or charges of which she was not aware because those charges were never disclosed in a timely manner allowing for dispute.

Jill Jones-Soderman, MSW, psychiatric social worker, PHD - psychoanalyst, MSHS - forensic expert in Law and Expert Witness Testimony:
Jill received her masters in Psychiatric Social Work at Hunter College School of Social Work in Manhattan, N.Y.
Jill's Doctorate in psychoanalysis was received from the
Institute for Advanced Training in Psychoanalysis and Psychotherapy via training at 3

institutes in Manhattan and New Jersey, though the primary accrediting institution was located in Haverstock England, the United Kingdom.. Her analyst was located in Woodcliff Lake New Jersey, Dr. William G. Herron., PhD. Dr. Herron certified in writing the number of hours Jill attended psychoanalysis which was approved by the analytic institute and by her New York State Social Work Licensing board which provided her with the highest level of clinical approval available. Interestingly, those who have attacked her doctoral training never contacted her psychoanalyst, a professor at St. John's University and resident of Woodcliff Lake New Jersey. Dr. Herron was a psychologist with four years of post graduate training in psychoanalysis at Adelphi University on Long Island.

Jill Jones-Soderman's control analysts (analytic supervisors) by whom she was supervised in Manhattan when she attended classes at the Columbia University College of Physicians included such luminaries as Dr. Otto Kernberg, MD, Dr. Michael Stone, MD, Dr. Lothar Gidro Frank, MD and Dr. Harold Searles, MD, among many other well known analysts. As she was an employee of New York State Psychiatric Institute, the state psychiatric training hospital for Columbia College of Physicians and Surgeons. The ignorance of those attempting to evaluate her level of training on the licensing board level did not even begin to have the depth of knowledge and training possessed by Jill Jones-Soderman and so could not begin to understand the depth and breadth of her training and the work or expense that went into her training; not that they ever asked or were

4

interested in such subjects. Her curriculum Vitae only begins to give a limited sense of the quality of her work or the respect for her talent which allowed her to be accepted into such a significant level of training. Documentation of her extensive training, teaching at schools of social work and at Columbia University College of Physicians and Surgeons are fully documented, were presented to the licensing boards and hang on her office walls.

There is unquestionably a witch hunt against Jill Jones-Soderman. The attempt to denigrate her training and talent, to discredit her skills in working as an expert witness before the courts has resulted in depriving hundreds of poor minority patients of their rights to regain their children, as Jill actively participated in a great deal of pro bono work and gave tirelessly of her talent to domestic violence and homeless shelters for men and women, working in a clinical capacity.

Jill has constantly challenged the authorities who attempted to use their power and control to transfer children from the hands of the protective parent into the hands of the abuser, as well as to tolerate integration of the wrongful use of pharmacology, and the failure to prohibit child trafficking and child abuse throughout the foster care system.

While Jill fought to create a record before licensing boards which targeted her, their deceitful manipulative tactics created an atmosphere in which it was impossible to convey or combat their overpowering message of control and ubiquitous superiority. To date, Jill Jones-Soderman refuses to have any connection to any licensing board, placing her client rights to privacy and due process as a n absolute priority. Her work as a Forensic Advocate provides a wide birth of activity and written and verbal expression for her. I am very pleased that Jill considers me a mentor, a supervisor as well as close friend and colleague.

Dr. Monty Weinstein

Document 11: Hearsay Commentary of Undercover Surveillance

There was no videorecording or audiorecording of this undercover operator's "findings." Only hearsay.

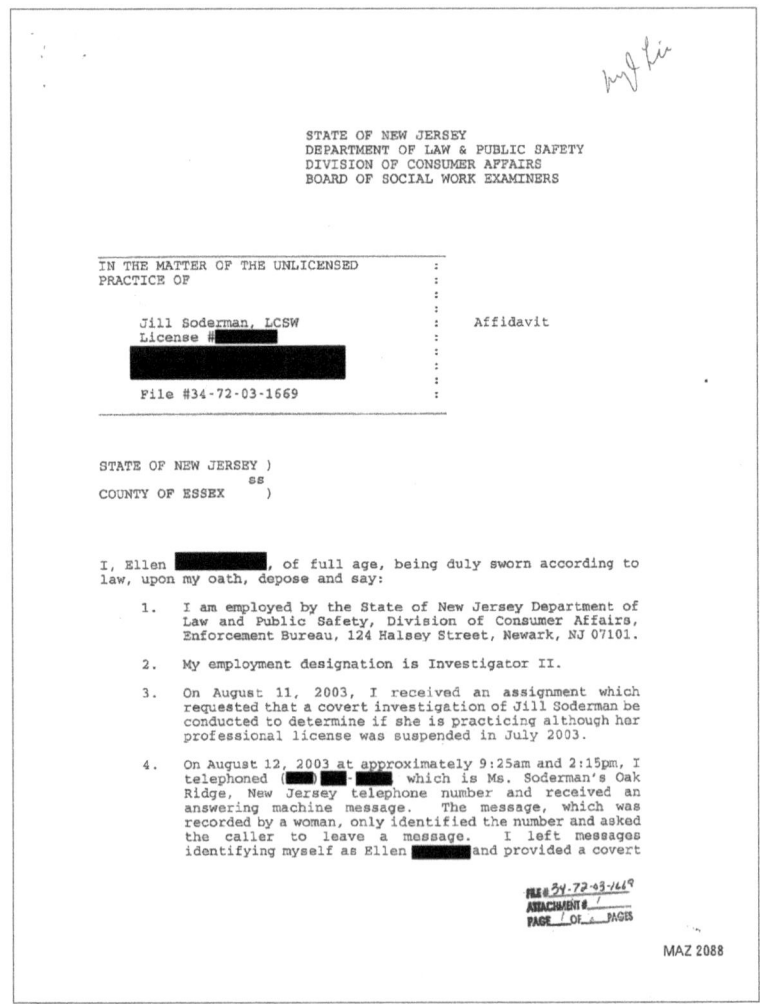

Page 2
File #34-72-03-1669
EP

telephone number during both telephone calls.

5. On August 13, 2003, at approximately 6:46pm Ms. Soderman left a voice mail message in response to the messages I had left for her on August 12, 2003. Ms. Soderman initially identified herself as "Jill Soderman" and then said "Dr. Soderman." Ms. Soderman stated that she would try calling again and provided (███) ███-████ as her telephone number.

6. On August 13, 2003, from approximately 7:05pm to 7:25pm, I received a telephone call from a woman who identified herself as Jill Soderman. In response, I asked if she was "Dr. Soderman." The woman answered "Yes," and began to ask about my personal problems and how I learned about her. I explained that I had recently divorced my husband, who had an affair. I felt alone because my sons live in San Diego and I have been staying with friends and cannot seem to motivate myself to get my life together and find a place to live. I further explained that my friend, Debbie, had found information on the Internet about some sort of conference held about a year ago that I believed had been sponsored by several attorneys and included her (Soderman) in the program. Ms. Soderman said that she speaks at many conferences and asked if I had any more information about the conference. When I said that I did not have the information with me, but recalled that the conference was held in Branchville, New Jersey, Ms. Soderman said the conference was sponsored by "F.I.T.-Families in Transition." I went on to say that my friend had urged me to attend the conference last year but I was too upset to attend because my divorce was "nasty."

Because my friend has continued to urge me to obtain help and I noted that the Internet information listed Ms. Soderman in Oak Ridge, I subsequently obtained her telephone listing and hoped she was the same person. Ms. Soderman said that her Oak Ridge home/office burned down last year and as a result she moved to a rental home in Sparta, New Jersey. However in June 2003, she moved to another home in Sparta located at ████████████████. She provided her Sparta phone number and explained that calls from her Oak Ridge telephone number are "remote call forwarded" to Sparta. [It should be noted that I had obtained Ms. Soderman's former and current addresses from the Sparta Post Office.] She provided directions to her home and said that the front door would be open and just

FILE # 34-72-03-1669
ATTACHMENT 6
PAGE 2 OF 6 PAGES

Page 3
File #34-72-03-1669
EP

come in.

During our conversation I addressed Ms. Soderman with the title of "Doctor" several times and was not corrected. When she offered to see me, I asked if she was available at about noon the next day. Ms. Soderman offered a 10:30am appointment and explained that she and her daughter had to be at Pope John High School, Sparta at noon and then /she had to be at the Morris County Detention Center at 1:00pm. I told her that I would try to get there at 10:30pm and would call if I would be late or could not make it. She asked why I had a problem with that time. I explained that I have had great difficulty sleeping at night and have been sleeping most mornings. In response, Ms. Soderman said that I was "depressed" and explained that there are different types of depression. After stating how difficult things have been, I asked if she could help me and how much she charged for her services. Ms. Soderman said that she recommends a minimum of three (3) sessions and charges $150.00 per visit. She indicated that there are ways to overcome depression and I could not do it without help.

7. On August 14, 2003, at approximately 10:25am, while Investigator John Musiello maintained surveillance, I arrived at Ms. Soderman's home and found the front door open and the screen/storm door unlocked. After ringing the bell and calling inside without getting a response, I entered the lake style house dining room and heard a man and a woman talking from the direction of the adjacent living room. I took Ms. Soderman's last business card from a dish near the front window. As I looked through the living room archways, to the right of the front door, I saw a woman reclining on a love seat against the wall of a small room just beyond the living room. During their discussion, I overheard the man address the woman as "Jill" while talking about his relationship problems. At approximately 10:30am, while escorting the man to the dining room, Ms. Soderman spoke about the aspects of a dysfunctional family. They tentatively scheduled his next visit for an evening later that week, which he would later confirm by telephone. As the man, who was about fifty (50) years old, approximately five (5) feet eight (8) inches tall, bald, trim build with broad shoulders and casually dressed, left through the front door, Ms. Soderman greeted me and invited me into her office, the room with the love seat. She sat and later reclined on the love seat during my

FILE # 34-72-03-1669
ATTACHMENT # ___
PAGE ___ OF ___ PAGES

visit. As we walked toward her office, her phone rang, as it did several times during the session. Her first conversation concerned a report she had drafted and promised to re-write and complete soon. Another call seemed to be from a concerned relative of a patient. I sat in one (1) of the two (2) chairs against the left wall of the room. There were many certificates covering the available wall space. Her New Jersey professional license was on a board and displayed on the desk to the right.

Ms. Soderman, who had dark straight short hair, appeared to be about fifty (50) years old, approximately five (5) feet four (4) inches tall, heavy set and casually dressed. Ms. Soderman did not ask me to complete a patient history form, nor did she take notes during our meeting.

The session began at about 10:40am with questions about my marital problems, family, and how long I had been feeling depressed. After discussing the problems of my twenty-five (25) years of marriage and approximate one (1) year of feeling depressed, Ms. Soderman asked if I had a doctor because I needed to take Zoloft (PLD) for my depression. She explained that the medication, which is very effective and would begin working in a day or two (2), would also help my insomnia. She offered to call Alexander Prezioso, M.D., a physician that she has asked to prescribe Zoloft for her patients. Ms. Soderman explained the benefits of the drug and need to begin taking the lowest dose of 25mg and possibly increase to the higher dosage of 100mg as needed. She said that I would not resolve my depression, which appeared to be a hormone problem in my brain, without the medication. She also said that if I preferred to see a physician other than the one Ms. Soderman recommended, she would gladly speak with that doctor about prescribing Zoloft, but asked that I provide the doctor with written authorization. She noted that Zoloft had minimal side effects and preferred it over most of the newer antidepressants. I said that I would think about calling a doctor and asked for Dr. Prezioso's business card. She did not have his card, but wrote the following information on a piece of pink paper and gave it to me:

"Dr. Alexander Preszioso [sic]-MD

Page 5
File #34-72-03-1669
EP

I also asked for her business card. She left the room and when she returned she said she discovered there were none left in the dining room and told me she had to have more printed as well as her stationery, with her new address.

I asked if she would be providing therapy while I took Zoloft and how long would I need to see her. She could not estimate how much therapy I would need, but explained that therapy consisted of talking about my problems while also taking the medication. Several times during the session Ms. Soderman said things that caused me concern which included telling me that I would become more and more depressed if I did not take Zoloft. She also told me that I would not ever become a functioning, independent person again if I did not take Zoloft. Just before leaving, Ms. Soderman suggested that I have my friend Debbie call her later that day. Ms. Soderman said that she believed I would not remember what we had discussed, and therefore, she would tell Debbie what is needed to overcome my depression.

I told her that my sons had some difficulty dealing with the divorce and asked if she would want to speak with them at some time. I prefaced this with her mentioning her appointment scheduled later that day at the Morris County Detention Center and asked if she saw young adults. Ms. Soderman explained that she is a forensic psychologist and evaluates prisoners and juveniles for the courts "all over," which included Morris, Sussex and Passaic Counties.

I gave Ms. Soderman $150.00 in cash for the session and requested a receipt. She explained that her stationery contained her previous Sparta address, which she crossed out and then wrote her new address. The receipt was not dated nor did it contain a diagnosis or patient name. Ms. Soderman signed her name without any titles and wrote: "Consultation, $150 Pd." However, her letterhead still contains, "PhD. Psychoanalysis and Psychotherapy." Because I told her that I was not certain that I had insurance coverage, I asked if she would submit claims for me. Ms. Soderman said that she would complete claims with the diagnosis and fees, but I would have to submit them for reimbursement.

I left at approximately 11:40am and traveled to a nearby location where I met with Inv. Musiello and recorded my

Page 6
File #34-72-03-1669
EP

recollection of the covert visit.

8. The original business card, the information about Dr. Prezioso, and the receipt are identified on Enforcement Bureau Evidence Voucher No. 093-03-34 as Item Nos. 1 through 3 respectively, and are being maintained in Evidence Storage. Photocopies of these items are attached and marked Exhibit Nos. 1 through 3, respectively.

I swear that all of the foregoing statements made by me are true. I am aware that if any of the foregoing statements are willfully false, I am subject to punishment.

Ellen ▇▇▇▇▇▇, Investigator

Sworn and subscribed to before me:
this 2nd Day of August, 2003

JEAN MURPHY
NOTARY PUBLIC OF NEW JERSEY
My Commission Expires Sept. 22, 2006

FILE # 34-72-03-1669
ATTACHMENT # 1
PAGE ___ OF ___ PAGES

State of New Jersey

OFFICE OF THE ATTORNEY GENERAL
DEPARTMENT OF LAW AND PUBLIC SAFETY
DIVISION OF CONSUMER AFFAIRS
STATE BOARD OF SOCIAL WORK EXAMINERS
124 HALSEY STREET, 6TH FLOOR, NEWARK NJ

JAMES E. MCGREEVEY
Governor

PETER C. HARVEY
Attorney General
RENI ERDOS
Director

August 19, 2003

Mailing Address:
P.O. Box 45033
Newark, NJ 07101
(973) 504-6495

Jill Soderman

RE: Compliance with the Terms of your Consent Order Filed on July 10, 2003.

Dear Ms. Soderman:

The New Jersey State Board of Social Work Examiners (the "Board") acknowledges receipt on August 18, 2003 of both portions of your New Jersey clinical social work license, in compliance with the Order you signed with the Board.

Please be reminded that the July 15, 2003 civil penalty payment of $676.00 as well as the August 15, 2003 payment of $676.00 are now immediately due and payable within 7 business days of the date of this correspondence, by August 28, 2003.

Very truly yours,

Kay K. McCormack
Executive Director

KKM:cc
cc: Marilyn Bair, DAG
    Stephen Scipione, Esq.

State of New Jersey

OFFICE OF THE ATTORNEY GENERAL
DEPARTMENT OF LAW AND PUBLIC SAFETY
DIVISION OF CONSUMER AFFAIRS
STATE BOARD OF SOCIAL WORK EXAMINERS
124 HALSEY STREET, 6TH FLOOR, NEWARK NJ

JAMES E. MCGREEVEY
Governor

PETER C. HARVEY
Attorney General
RENI ERDOS
Director

August 19, 2003

Mailing Address:
P.O. Box 45033
Newark, NJ 07101
(973) 504-6495

Jill Soderman

RE: Compliance with the Terms of your Consent Order Filed on July 10, 2003.

Dear Ms. Soderman:

The New Jersey State Board of Social Work Examiners (the "Board") acknowledges receipt on August 18, 2003 of both portions of your New Jersey clinical social work license, in compliance with the Order you signed with the Board.

Please be reminded that the July 15, 2003 civil penalty payment of $676.00 as well as the August 15, 2003 payment of $676.00 are now immediately due and payable within 7 business days of the date of this correspondence, by August 28, 2003.

Very truly yours,

Kay K. McCormack
Executive Director

KKM:cc
cc: Marilyn Bair, DAG
    Stephen Scipione, Esq.

New Jersey Is An Equal Opportunity Employer • Printed on Recycled Paper and Recyclable

State of New Jersey

OFFICE OF THE ATTORNEY GENERAL
DEPARTMENT OF LAW AND PUBLIC SAFETY
DIVISION OF CONSUMER AFFAIRS
STATE BOARD OF SOCIAL WORK EXAMINERS
124 HALSEY STREET, 6TH FLOOR, NEWARK NJ

JAMES E. MCGREEVEY
Governor

PETER C. HARVEY
Attorney General
RENI ERDOS
Director

August 19, 2003

Mailing Address:
P.O. Box 45033
Newark, NJ 07101
(973) 504-6495

Jill Soderman

RE: Compliance with the Terms of your Consent Order Filed on July 10, 2003.

Dear Ms. Soderman:

The New Jersey State Board of Social Work Examiners (the "Board") acknowledges receipt on August 18, 2003 of both portions of your New Jersey clinical social work license, in compliance with the Order you signed with the Board.

Please be reminded that the July 15, 2003 civil penalty payment of $676.00 as well as the August 15, 2003 payment of $676.00 are now immediately due and payable within 7 business days of the date of this correspondence, by August 28, 2003.

Very truly yours,

Kay K. McCormack
Executive Director

KKM:cc
cc: Marilyn Bair, DAG
    Stephen Scipione, Esq.

New Jersey Is An Equal Opportunity Employer • Printed on Recycled Paper and Recyclable

Document 12: Mother's Signed Release

Soderman

To Whom This May Concern,

From February 2001, and until present day I have given my permission, both orally and in writing to Jill Soderman. To discuss with whomever she deemed necessary in reference to assisting my children and I.

This authorization was not defined to any particular person or agency, but, as per her discretion of whomever she felt was necessary to speak to.

Respectfully,

Danielle   3/20/02

Danielle   , 3/20/02.

Document 13: Article About Mary Margaret McVeigh

An article in PR Newswire about the corrupt practices of Judge Mary Margaret McVeigh.

APPENDIX

breaking business news - national business news - world business ne... http://www2.prnewswire.com/cgi-bin/stories.pl?ACCT=AZCALL.st...

Business

New Jersey Judge Under Fire for Alleged Corruption

NYACK, N.Y., Oct. 13 /PRNewswire/ -- A New Jersey Superior Court Judge is coming under fire from a wide array of victims and their families, some of whom have filed lawsuits alleging violations of their civil rights, racketeering, elder abuse and severe unethical behavior, among other crimes.

In one of the more recent cases, Judge Mary Margaret McVeigh is accused of sentencing 86-year-old Blanche Zwerdling to live in nursing home - against her wishes and those of her family - to ostensibly gain control of her trust fund and bank accounts. Full details can not yet be disclosed because the case and a potential investigation are ongoing, but further reports will follow.

According to a family member and court documents, the judge appointed three $300 per hour lawyers for Zwerdling - one as a guardian - while she was placed involuntarily in an assisted-living facility in New Jersey. In addition, her money is being wasted by the court while her health deteriorates, the family member said.

"My mother in law was so happy and comfortable in Florida," said her son-in-law. "Is this how you protect her? Spend her money without discretion, and say in open court: 'she has it so we can spend it.'"

Her grandson, who was the lawful trustee of the trust, was illegally removed without explanation, according to the son-in-law. The court-appointed guardian was subsequently put in charge. The granddaughter who had lived with and cared for the woman for seven years, was thrown out on the street while the judge slapped her with a restraining order. No family members are allowed to speak with the elderly woman about her situation. And over $200,000 has been drained from her bank account by the court and the three lawyers so far, while many of her belongings were discarded at the whim of her "guardian."

Speaking to investigators, another son-in-law accused McVeigh of illegal eviction, illegal separation, illegal takeover of a trust, violation of the right to choose an attorney, failing to provide an accounting of the money that was being spent and even refusal to allow an assessment of the property after the unlawful eviction. The judge is also facing allegations of a conflict of interest in the case. Susan Champion, the court-appointed guardian, is allegedly a "very close friend" of McVeigh, the son told investigators. "It makes me think back to Nazi Geasmany," he added.

This is far from the first case that has called McVeigh's ethics and behavior into question.

She was recently named as a defendant in an ongoing federal civil rights action by Jill Jones-Soderman, the Executive Director of the Foundation for the Child Victims of the Family Courts and an accomplished author, speaker and social worker. According to Jones-Soderman, the judge's suppression of evidence and corrupt decision making led to the suicide of a 12-year-old boy, who was transferred by the court into the hands of his alleged abuser.

"Judge McVeigh is using her position to ruin innocent victims and enrich herself and her cronies, so I decided to put a stop to this using the federal courts," said Jones-Soderman, who was also targeted by the judge. "The number of complaints keeps rising, so eventually the truth about her activities will be known and justice will be served," she added.

Another victim of Judge McVeigh was Antonio Latona Sr., according to reports, his family and court documents. After suffering a stroke, he was left partially handicapped, but with the support and assistance of his children, he decided to continue living in Florida with one of his daughters to care for him, where he made friends, continued his gardening and enjoyed the beach.

Against the advice of doctors, social workers, lawyers and other medical experts, the judge ordered him confined to a nursing home in New Jersey. In the 60 days that he spent in the state, he was hospitalized three times. Ultimately, he began suffering from multiple ailments and passed away in September of 2008.

"My father was murdered by that woman," said Antonio Latona Jr., a New Jersey man who claims that Judge McVeigh lied, suppressed evidence and used intimidation in the case. He is also in the midst of litigation. "I will spend the rest of my life to expose her every chance I get. People need to know what she has done and what she continues to do - she has to be stopped from destroying lives on a daily basis."

If you or somebody you know has been harmed by Judge McVeigh and her rulings, please visit http://www.tonylatona.com for more information.

Document 14: Email Correspondences for A Yellow Ribbon for H

Emails between Kelly, the head of the organization, and H's mother regarding their fight for sole custody.

> 02/01/07
> J Meier to KS
>
> KS:
>
> I'm thrilled to hear that the new GAL report gives you almost half time with Holden. I agree with Michael Lesher that this is such a huge step forward that I feared would never come. Best of luck in taking that step and moving forward and better from there. If family courts actually recognized abuse when it was happening we would not be in this place. But they don't, so getting half time (or close) is hugely important and lays the foundation for further reversals in the future. I hope it works that way for you.
>
> Best, Joan

[Handwritten note:] There was no reversal. His mother never saw her son again. May — 2018

02/03/07
KS to JJS

Dear KS,

I know you are angry and outraged and you have every right to be! Please take a breath and listen to me.

The Judge brought me into chambers after M˙ was hurt the 2nd time. She said I will give you full custody but you have to allow him unsupervised visits ever other weekend. I said so when she gets hurt again it will be my fault and not yours. I said NO!

She gave my ex full physical and legal. Me supervised visits. Ironically there was no talk of supervised visits for J˙ ˙. I live with the nightmare of my decision every day. I never thought by not doing what the Judge requested she would turn the wrath of her power on me. Crippling me.

These are very disturbed people. I now realize it would be better for M˙ to be with me and mistreated every other weekend, then the situation I have now. I blame myself every day for not taking that offer. All I could think of was going back to "Mommy please don't make me go and see Daddy he hurts my bottom." The agony of it, I just couldn't bear it and it would be my fault because I agreed to it.

Please learn from the agony of my decision. They also gave me visitation during the week when M˙ was to be in pre-school. I kept her home. To spend the time I had left with her before they took her. Now you are expected to take him to daycare instead of caring for him in your home.

I know your pain and I understand everything you are feeling. Agreeing means it never happened. Agreeing means allowing them to sweep it under the rug. At the time I did what I thought was right. Black and White, bright and wrong.

Please give yourself some time. Lets talk. I made what I thought was the right decision. One of character and integrity. "What your asking is for me to say it is OK for him to abuse her every other weekend. That's great! Then your off the hook!" Then it is my fault because I agreed.

Please take a breath. Lets talk. I replay that day over and over in my mind. More so since we met. Seeing you living my nightmare. Like my suffering was for nothing. You are in my thoughts and prayers.

Peace and Love,
Kelly Fink

02/04/07
KS to JJS

This is the punishment Lyons slapped me with for reporting the sexual abuse of my son by his father.

Garland Waller of Small Justice Responds

With legal custody and primary physical custody to remain with father, he and his father's rights lawyer Mary Socha are given the power to ensure H   gets set on in therapy by another Pilachowski. Again I am asked to come up with 'names' of possible therapists, just as I was asked to come up with names of possible people to supervise my visits with H   , to make it appear as if I had an input, when in actuality it was already a forgone conclusion through collusion with Socha, famous for arranging that courthouse around the father's demands.

H   is a year overdue for therapy, he is depressed and aggressive, written up by the nun Susan Goldstein of the Sisters of St. Joseph as having behavioral problems. She's been 'teaching' him since mid September, has never met his father, and thinks his grandmother may be dropping H   off.

I want to do nothing that allows anyone to think that it's okay now to allow K   to continue to molest our son if it's only three days a week.

Don says he needs to know what my bottom line is so he can negotiate with Socha.

It is written right on the P.A.C.T. (Parents And Children in Transition) handbook, the course that divorcing parents are required by the Sate of Mass to complete before a divorce is granted, page seventeen:

"Parents Who Are Not Capable: It is unfortunate but true that not all adults are capable of parenting. When there is a history of *physical, verbal, emotional or sexual abuse*, alcohol or drug abuse; or menta illness, it may be in the child's best interest to have no contact or limited and monitored contact with that parent."

K   's visitation needs to be limited and monitored as it has been in the past. The judge was removed for her poor decision in Holden's case. I have every reason to expect a reversal. That's my bottom line.

Kathy Lee Scholpp and a Yellow Ribbon for Holden

----- Original Message -----
From:
To:
Sent:
Subject:

Dear Kathy:

I got a short message from Don Frank indicating that the Cavellero report is in. Although he couldn't tell me much (it's about 70 pages), he did summarize her recommendations, which I found VERY encouraging. I do want to see the report itself, of course, but that's going to be a bit complicated, since he ask for court permission, etc. So for the moment, let's go on what I know.

Working the sort of cases I do, I know how to distinguish good, indifferent, bad and very bad. (I've left out the REALLY good, because that seldom needs explaining or nuancing.) in my cases, mothers all too often face total ruptures of their relationships with their children, or get at most supervised visitation for a couple of hours per week. It's hard to exaggerate the anguish of a mother who has raised a small child full-time to find herself reduced to such a state, particularly when she knows the child needs her – needs her time, her presence, her (his) home, and an open setting (not a supervised clinical room) in which to relate.

So I can appreciate the big positive step this report seems to offer. It's MUCH better than what most mothers get in your circumstances, and it gives you room both to develop your relationship with Holden and to offer him protection for the future.

I did not and could not expect that a G.A.L. working under the prior orders in this case was going to announce to the court that, contrary to all previous findings, the child was abused and should be isolated from the father, etc. But in giving you four out of seven overnights and NO supervision, the G.A.L. is effectively acknowledging that there's nothing wrong with you, your mind or your desire to help H   . Better still, the absence of supervision prevents court personnel from manipulating him or your relationship, or interfering in whatever he wants or needs to say to you. And the time you'll have with him will effectively prevent alienation tactics.

So the good news is that if the judge follows the recommendations, supervisors will be out of your life, and you'll have Holden more than half the overnights and, I take it, most of the time That's a whole lot better than where we are, and a very good place to begin the important work of repairing your relationship – which is central in importance for his welfare and safety as well as your rights. Of course, the judge may not g along . . . but at the moment, I'm optimistic.

Of course, the new (modified) order doesn't prevent us from appealing in an attempt to bring back the former arrangement, particularly as to legal custody . . .but again, we'll be in a MUCH strengthened position and have much less to lose from an affirmance. Since appeals are low-percentage undertakings, I consider that another very important and positive factor in the current report.

Also, the G.A.L. recommends that H   have therapy, which I think is another good thing, since it gives him a neutral professional to talk to about any problems or fears. And that takes presser off YOU if there are any concerns.

As I understand it, the other side of the coin – there usually is one, in the law business – is that you aren't supposed to question or talk to H   about the abuse allegations. That, too, is to be expected at this stage. – and frankly I don't see any real harm in it. The past discussions are all matters of record: nothing will change them. At this point, even a sympathetic abuse expert would advise to avoid further questioning, especially by non-professionals. That's because reporting means less and less in the legal system the more the child is questioned. It is believed that repeated questioning distorts the child's responses, so that by this time asking him ore questions wouldn't do us any good, because we could only traverse old territory with diminishing results. On the contrary, it would hurt us, because the fact of the questioning could be used against you while, as I said, not helping us a bit. So this restriction is a price we'll hardly feel. And I think it's offset by giving H   a therapist, who will not be under such restrictions, if the subject needs to be explored.

I know this doesn't satisfy all our needs or address all our questions. But this is the real world, and Family Court, as you already know, is far from the best even that mass of compromises usually has to offer. Mothers in your position are often fighting just to see their kids at all.

Therefore, I'm cautiously optimistic about the whole of this report, and very optimistic about its basic recommendations, which I think help us far more than they hurt us. Most of all, they help H   , and that's the most important thing of all. Child sexual abuse is one of the hardest things to prove, and it's rare case of mine that ever gets to that point. In fact, I can't think of one at the moment. What I aim for is 1)undo the punitive damage done to mothers trying to protect their children in good faith, and 2) rebuild the relationship between mother and child so that the child is properly protected. Most of the time that's the best the court system offers a mother who suspects sex abuse but can't et proof the courts will accept. And we try all we can to establish conditions that will deter any problems – verbal, boundary violations, whatever – for the future.

I think we're moving in all those directions here.

Now, the next step, of course, is to see that the judge approves the recommendations. Then you, Don and I must see where we stand regarding an appeal. I take it we'll still have a challenge to make, based on legal custody if nothing else. But this is certainly much preferable to an appeal from an order leaving you with nothing but short supervised visits, while your relationship dwindles into nothing and court personnel take over your life.

If you know anything more about the report, please let me know. Meanwhile, stay in touch, and keep praying. So far we've certainly escaped the worst.

Michael

P.S.: I've spoken to Jill Jones but didn't realize you knew her. We've consulted regarding another case of mine in which the mother is accused of physical abuse.

Michael Lesher, Esq.
mlesher@att.net
www.michaellesher.com
(973) 470-0212 Joan S Meigher, Esqu., Professor of Clinical Law
Director, Domestic Violence Legal Empowerment and Appeals Project
George Washington University Law School
2000 G St. N.W., Washington, D.C. 20052
(202) 994-2278 (ph)
(202)994-4946 (fax)
jmeier@law.gwu.edu

Milton Keynes UK
Ingram Content Group UK Ltd.
UKHW040722161023
430697UK00001B/123